Value in Marx

Value in Marx

*The Persistence of Value
in a More-Than-Capitalist World*

George Henderson

University of Minnesota Press

Minneapolis · London

The publication of this book was supported by an Annual Award from the University of Minnesota Provost's Office, Imagine Fund for the Arts, Design, and Humanities.

Published by the University of Minnesota Press
111 Third Avenue South, Suite 290
Minneapolis, MN 55401-2520
http://www.upress.umn.edu

Library of Congress Cataloging-in-Publication Data

Henderson, George L.
  Value in Marx : the persistence of value in a more-than-capitalist world / George Henderson.
  Includes bibliographical references and index.
  ISBN 978-0-8166-8095-5 (hc : alk. paper)
  ISBN 978-0-8166-8096-2 (pb : alk. paper)
1. Marxian economics. 2. Value. 3. Marx, Karl, 1818–1883. I. Title.
  HB97.5.H425   2013
  335.4'12--dc23

2012049134

Printed in the United States of America on acid-free paper

The University of Minnesota is an equal-opportunity educator and employer.

20 19 18 17 16 15 14 13   10 9 8 7 6 5 4 3 2 1

Contents

Acknowledgments

If ever a book was privileged by good friendship and conversation, this is it. My deep appreciation goes to Bruce Braun and Vinay Gidwani, intrepid supporters and faithful challengers many years in and out, and to Tracey Deutsch and Karen Ho, stalwart comrades and fellow conveners of the generative Markets in Time research collaborative at the Institute for Advanced Study at the University of Minnesota. I am eternally grateful to the good folks who posed the right questions of the book, in whole or in part, or who simply planted in my mind essential turns of thought, at just the right moments: Vinay Gidwani, Marv Taylor, Bruce Braun, Morgan Adamson, the reviewers commissioned by the University of Minnesota Press, and Jason Weidemann, my editor at the University of Minnesota Press. Jason's enthusiasm has been exceptional and the press's staff terrific to work with—Mike Hanson, Dani Kasprzak, Alicia Sellheim, Anne Wrenn, and others who do the good work of making books possible, I am indebted to you. Sabbatical and fellowship leaves were instrumental, and I owe thanks to the Department of Geography, the Institute for Advanced Study, and the Faculty Sabbatical Supplement Fund, all at the University of Minnesota. Because a book is always more than the story it supposes itself to be, the work, hope, and dreams represented here are forever stamped by the love and kindness of my parents, my brother, my sister, and the circle of extraordinary friends upon whom I've leaned in the last couple of years. There is one person for whom no acknowledgment can be too great: my son Simon, Mr. Bones, my heart. This Marx is for you.

Introduction

Did Marx Have a Theory of Value?

The theory of value, readers of Karl Marx know, occupies a prominent place in his writings and his politics. This is so because it is capitalism to which value seems most attached: capitalism taking Marx's world by storm, value being the predominant lever for the study of political economy in his day. Where capitalism would rudely heap everything on the market, from bibles to whiskey, and where the self-same dollar could buy passage to heaven or hell, as it were, and in the bargain upend the difference, *value* would coolly reveal the equivalences holding this chaotic jumble together—this "immense collection of commodities" through which wealth appears in capitalist society, as Marx puts it on the first page of *Capital*. But this same value, in Marx's rendering, also would explain the exact opposite, the inequivalence holding things together: the inequality that miraculously emerges from equality, as when profit seems to magically appear from fair-market exchange, like gold from straw. Marx's struggle to be persuasive on the question of value—to respond to its conundrums by focusing on labor time and the difference between labor and labor power and, scandalously, to assert the core insolvency of the immense collection—is fought tooth and nail.

Eager heir to the long history of questions concerning the properties of value and its labyrinthine acreage of allied ideas (commodities, money, and prices; uses, exchanges, and desires), Marx takes possession of this inheritance not as a demurring caretaker tends to a grand estate but as a wrecking ball takes to an ailing, jerry-rigged mansion. From every side, he lets the ball loose, knocking holes in the rickety ideas and hobbled dreams

of bourgeois political economy, most of all those shoddy notions of value that legitimate poverty amid plenty, manufactured
need amid the possibility of real need, and stunted human being amid the potential for holistic development and that undercut the human spirit with grinding labor yet resurrect the false
piety of hard work. Every destructive blow against orthodoxy
is, however, also a rebuilding. Across hundreds and hundreds
of pages of text, a mansion of his own, perhaps, Marx remodels
the choked and occluded site of value into what he considers a
science (the first) of capitalism. Such is value in Marx's hands,
an idea he killed so that it could live, even while he himself did
not live to finish the job.

But it also is right there in the act of construction where the
important questions begin. What does value live for in Marx? Is
its role exclusively that of a critical science of capitalism? Or
does it have ulterior constructive content—is the end of capitalism the end of value? And does he have a single theory of value
that serves all of his destructive and reconstructive purposes?
My intent here is to explore what can be thought of as the lives
of value in Marx's work, lives that are caught up in the capitalist
moment but also take up residence beyond it. In writing "lives,"
I therefore signal both a distance from the idea that what Marx
comes up with in his struggle against orthodoxy is *a* theory of
value and a usefulness served by maintaining that distance. Pin-
ning Marx to a single such theory whose provenance and power
is best restricted to an analysis of capital and its law, as the dominant readings are wont to do, is too restrictive, akin to snatching
a single frame from a series of moving images. In the rereading
of Marx I offer here, my hope is that value emerges as a livelier,
more persistent, and more relevant figure than is captured by
the conceptual or historical equation between capital and value.
The call to break this equation, apart from the interest such a
reading might have on its own terms—genuine enough, since to
really read is to really *think*—comes from the fact that Marx's
value-theoretic investments structure not only his critique of
capital but also the way he thinks about capital's beyond. These
investments are at the center of the critique of capitalism, but his
critique of contemporary socialist and communist experiments

depend on them, too. And this is not only because these experiments sometimes repeat the errors of capitalist value relations but because, in my reading, Marx seeks a positive valence for value-theoretic investments as such. More than anything, it is this dimension of Marx's investments that bring them into the light of today. Why? Insofar as capitalism is not bound to last (is the passing of modes of production not at least one lesson of history's long durée?), as the need for something better always-already is palpable and as capitalism anyway is shot through with logics beyond its own, these wider value-theoretic horizons of Marx remain eminently worthy of study.

There is a certain rowing against the tide in a rereading that proposes to break the value–capital couplet. Marx's own characterizations of value as something relevant to all forms of production, let alone capitalism, are not easy to assimilate. They apparently sit so uneasily with the overwhelming, mainline attention he gives to deploying value in the diagnosis of capitalism that the elasticity of value perennially seems to snap back into that comfortable role. But capital and value are an overlapping, not mutually exclusive set, and Marx scores, in my reading anyway, a number of important political points by keeping them apart. This is the initial sense of the idea, then, that Marx does not have *a* theory of value. But the picture is also more complicated than just that. For there is no one theory of value that can be said to include Marx's theory of capital and then extend beyond it. The larger goal then would be to etch in the idea that value is multiple, not singular, in Marx's oeuvre and to assemble a picture of how so. Anyone with at least an initial sense of *the* theory of value, perhaps gained from the first volume of *Capital*, probably senses that I am making something of a gamble (even though certain points made herein have been made by others at other times). I want to suggest that for those curious as to what value is, we get closer to the truth of the matter by *not* finding problematic its multiple appearances and *by* finding a new political imaginary in those multiples.

But already, there is a need to halt a certain regress. If Marx's value is not reducible to what capital circulates—inverting David Harvey's formulation in *Limits to Capital* that capital is the circulation of value—and if it is not a single theory, what is it? To be a little too bloodless about it, value can be thought of as the name for how productive, social activities get divided up within societies, activities—labor, in the very broadest sense—that yield the assemblages of humans and nonhumans that are necessary to sustain life, as well as spark new life. This is the essential point Marx draws his onetime friend Ludwig Kugelmann's attention to in a revealing letter (I reproduce key passages from the letter at the start of chapter 5). This is not the same as saying Marx has a single value theory after all, only that the concept of value creates an object/problem that it works on. The theoretical substance is, then, in the details of how the relations and processes that compose and recompose assemblages actually work themselves out. Marx himself variously works upon the problem as he attends to these different compositions, including, though not exclusively, those of capitalism. That said, these variations gather around the fault line of whether the problem of dividing productive activities in a balanced sort of way either is solvable—and if so, how—or is likely to remain a problem and maybe even ought to remain a problem—and if so, why.

The play of value as problem and value as solution, an entirely too simplistic formulation, but sufficing as a way in, is of enormous interest. For example, reading across a diversity of Marx's work, we can see him making the case that the messy matter of dividing up labor expenditures potentially is, in fact, its own solution. That is, it is in the historical and contradictory nature of capitalism that the way in which the problem of value unfolds as a "fraternization of impossibilities" creates possibilities, but not guarantees, for its later solution.[1] Famously, proper passage through capitalism might potentially set up society with various resources and a radical consciousness to devise a balanced division of labor expenditures. This hope for a future predicated on associated production is, I think, what gets Marx saying that, on the one hand, value does not really exist in capitalism but could really exist, on the other, in associated production. It depends on which window is being looked through. Thus, it is *sort of true* that value exists only in associated production, but it is *also* sort of true that value exists in capitalism. Marx—as I read him in parts 1 and 2 of this work—just insists on having it both ways: value conceived as a problem but also as a problem that might be solvable. But it also is important to note that these windows, so to speak, cannot be fused into a larger opening, because there is no guarantee the problem can be solved. I caution that this is a simplified version of the actual arguments I make. For example, it is possible to read Marx additionally saying that value does not appear in capitalism even on capital's own terms. But this is part of the same logic of problem/solution just alluded to, the special case of capitalism being that it cannot evince the problem of value clearly; it is occluded by a proxy—namely, money. Money, Marx shows, makes it impossible and indeed *unnecessary* to actually extract, as such, the question of the social division of productive activities, which is to say—so as to pump some blood into the matter—the question of the production of social life itself is, in capitalism, not needed. (This is great news if you happen to be a Wall Street banker, but it should leave everyone else feeling scandalized and cheated.)

To say Marx does not have *a* theory of value is not to then attempt a textbook-like enumeration of some number of different theories of value he has. (Nor do I hope to be taken for wading into the thicket where strict definitions of theories, concepts, and differences between them abide.) The point I want to make is that value fails to coalesce in a single way. It is disrupted by a fault line and for this reason will never be bound to fully satisfy. But this failure of course is where all the vitality is, or so I have come to conclude. It is possible to read value in Marx as a *capitalist* problem meant to go away (a reading I treat but am more critical of), a problem meant to be solved, or a problem meant to remain a problem, and it certainly is possible to read Marx as being value theoretic in ways he likely does not necessarily mean but are nonetheless available.

Several implications follow. The first is that value and capitalism are indeed not forever joined. There is, despite a long, entrenched tradition of reading Marx that states the opposite, a disunity between them, a disunity that invites not only the

question of the delimited durée of capitalism but also the inces-
sant renewal of the value lever. (This is a particular point of
chapters 1 and 2.) But as the matter is ever more closely approached it accrues even greater interest and relevance. And
so there is a second implication. Marx's exploration of how and
why capital and value are not coterminous—a fragmented exploration across a number of different texts—is absolutely fateful for his hope that value can properly emerge as a solution,
so to speak, in associated production. By "fateful," I mean that
Marx identifies a set of issues in his critique of capitalism that
he never convincingly resolves when he invokes value in a postcapitalist key. By this, I mean that his own overt suggestions
for value as solution, if I can continue to put it that way, tend
toward being ideological, as when certain faults of capitalism
identified in his critique turn up unexamined when he thinks
value in postcapitalist associated production. This is the point
of chapters 3 and 4, which culminate in an examination of the
identity Marx tries to establish between freedom and free time.
The real freedom that begins only after the production of needs
has been met, an assertion of Marx, has the unfortunate effect
of splitting production into two realms, one abject, the other
not. He would have to explain just why anyone would want to
undertake abjected activity. (I suggest how he might do this.)
This problem is compounded by a question that emerges in the
first two chapters: whether it is believable that the associated
production Marx holds out for us would not produce out of itself some sort of developmental limit or barrier, an "independent social power" (as Marx claims of money in the commodity
society). What these difficulties mean is that the questions Marx
raises about capitalism's handling of value never really go away,
and we cannot not think about this (I cannot, anyway) when he
gets around to positing value in associated production. What
can we do with this impasse? Is it fatal that Marx's critique-cum-
construction is self-tainting?

I address these questions in chapter 5 by drawing out a third
implication of the fault line that cuts through the different modalities of value. This chapter suggests that the impasse Marx
produces can be usefully dealt with by engaging his fascination

with how social power gets expressed in "things" and, as we posit a desired form of production beyond capitalism, by actually *valuing the limit* that things pose to the field of social potentialities. The chapter is built, in other words, around a possibility, mentioned earlier in passing, that it might be reasonable to keep value as problem alive. The chapter, while titled a "hypothesis," offers not a *sole* thought as to how to do this but rather a thought process, a thinking. That is—and here I again recall something mentioned earlier in passing—the chapter imputes that the meanings and species of the value concept inhere not in a still, captured frame but in motion, in dynamic ensemble within and without capitalism. This means that the issue of value in Marx does not devolve to which modality of value is truest so much as it devolves to the questions and prompts that these different explorations of value pose to each other.

These matters are brought to light in chapter 5 through an examination of Marx's fascination, repeated in all his value-theoretic explorations, with the expression of social power via things. This fascination strongly emerges in his analysis of the commodity fetish, of course. But the fetish makes, I suggest, a radical return in his work. An essential difficulty and opportunity for readers who want to explore the political qualities of value is that Marx is unable to part company with the idea that a single sort of thing can come to stand for the universality of social processes. In capitalism this thing is money; in associated production Marx toys with the notion that it could be the body of the producers themselves. The single thing is significant for Marx because it marks and becomes the measure of what counts as universality, where universality stands for the potential of something to become other than what it is, to enter into relations other than those that prevail at a given moment. Labor and labor time are "well spent" if universality in this sense is promoted in the process. (Thus, in capitalism money-thing is the master facilitator of commodity exchange in which all manner of socially produced use values are ripped out of their contexts and placed into new ones. In associated production the body-thing of the producers is, because it spends its labors well, the master thing equipped to produce freely across any sector of production and perhaps equally free to cross the boundary between productive time and free time, rather than having the boundary imposed.) I argue that Marx gives us reason to think—though he avoids thinking so overtly and formulaically—that it would be dangerous to deny the emergence of such a thing, even beyond capital. In sum, Marx's political and social imaginary is steeped in fascination with how social relations and their potential universality manifest physically (money, body, etc.), steeped in fascination with social relations that even if they could be "just right," nonetheless are in need of some sort of objectification, of an identifiable marker, a fixity. (Marx *claims* communism knows itself and needs no measure, but then he cannot resist pointing to the communist body-thing as *how we know it*.) But equally to the point is that once Marx's fascination is spotted, it is easy to posit that these very manifestations are, precisely because they are thingly, a limit or constraint on universality, on what else could be, on what other relations could be entered into. Marx develops precisely this analysis of money (as I show in chapters 1 and 2), yet I am also saying (per chapters 3 and 4) that there is very little keeping us from positing some similar constraints in the case of producer-bodies. To give all of this a turn of phrase, Marx's ruminations on value as problem (the messy matter of how labor is expended across society) utterly haunt value as potential solution (the possibility of balanced expenditure), though he never says so directly and *sometimes seems to say the opposite*. I do not see this as a bad haunting.

These arguments set up the necessary question of whether Marx ever does explicitly value the production of a thing because it is uniquely charged with the power to expose the limits of universality, such that it is not simply universality that is prized but also the signification that shows the limited way in which universality is produced in a given social setting. This is precisely the case I make for Marx's well-known assessment of Greek art at the end of the introduction to the *Grundrisse*, the name given to his extensive notebooks made in preparation for *Capital*. Marx makes the interesting assertion that Greek art could have been produced only by the ancient Greeks but that this context fails to account for the object itself. Greek art is underdetermined by its context. It is surpassing; it is the site of matter revealed otherwise than the context in which it circulates. (Nota bene, the thought is faintly echoed on the very first page of the first chapter of *Capital*, where Marx notes that commodities, as formed matter, always have other potential uses that would be accounted for by neither their "use value" nor their circulation as "exchange values." Commodities are lively with unattributed, as-yet-unnamed matter.) That is to say, Greek art's unique power is, in Marx's reckoning, that it goes beyond the universality (in the aforementioned sense) of its time; it exposes and indeed unveils the limits of universality as it emerged in ancient Greece. Marx, in my reading, is enchanted with Greek art having this nonintegrated relation to its situation and, crucially, urges a "higher development" of this principle, essentially ushering in a notion of the good fetish—hence, the claim of the radical return of the fetish. Yet shrewdly, Marx councils that even though Greek art is from a historical perspective, a peak of artistic production, it is an "unattainable norm."

The higher development of Greek art urged by Marx, which is of long-standing interest to Marxist cultural and literary theorists, has wider relevance. Grasped as a provocative concern with difference and limits, it can productively join the ensemble of value thought in Marx and productively confront the impasse toward which this ensemble points by, as it were, turning the impasse on its head while not pretending to erase it. Thus, if the things in which social becoming is invested can pose limits to that becoming, then it also is possible to affirm that these limits can be valued in positive terms—by using the tools of Marx's sensibilities, thinking carefully about what "unattainable norm" might mean, and dropping the pretense of having achieved utopia. Through a reading of Marx's reading of Greek art, a solution to the value problem opens up: keep value *as a problem* alive rather than trying to kill it off. In other words find and prize those social objects that neither confirm nor reflect the prevailing arrangements for how labor expenditures are distributed but rather expose their limits, manifest other possibilities and objectives for individual and social becoming, and indicate the pleasures of nonplenary longings—value *those* things and the manner in which they arise.

Why does any of this stuff matter? In contrast with many other engagements with value theory, the main concern of this book is not with the workings of the law of value in contemporary (or historical) capitalism and the new forms it is taking. The main concern is to draw upon Marx's engagements with value, which inevitably draw in his concern with capitalism, as well as much broader sensibilities, and to adduce a political imaginary of value for societies where capitalism prevails but where it is thought this might not forever be so.

It is time to write something about certain mainline ways of studying Marx's handling of value that I have avoided, despite being respectful of them. I have not waded into those classic problems that try to reconcile market prices, wages, and profits, all ostensibly surface appearances, with value as a deeper structure (i.e., value narrowly regarded as units of socially necessary labor time employed in commodity production). One of these kinds of reconciliations is the so-called transformation problem, through which the attempt is made to explain why the surplus value generated by capitalist firms during production is typically not reflected in the actual profits they receive as a result of market exchange (i.e., the transformation of values into so-called prices of production). Whether this problem can be solved and, if so, under what conditions has in some circles been the reason to accept Marx's analysis of capitalism or drop it altogether. Another classic I avoid is the reduction problem: On what basis can "complex" labor, such as scientific research in a pharmaceutical company or decision making in a health insurance corporation or the laborious writing of algorithms for a software firm, be quantitatively compared with "simple" labor like scanning bar codes at a supermarket or a loading dock, as if so many hours of complex labor could be considered the equivalent of so many hours of simple labor? These conundrums, which remain as lively as ever, are not my specific training, though they leave aside broader questions that also are of interest.[2]

I have been more drawn to an influential interpretation of value by Diane Elson in her indispensable 1978 essay "The Value Theory of Labor." Her view is adopted by the lineage to which I trace my own affinities (especially, David Harvey and his students, though in their estimation I may herein fall far from the tree!). Elson's interpretation, which is not hers alone of course, is more interested in value as an argument for what happens and what problems arise when wage labor is the predominant form of labor, including why value even needs to be expressed in the form of money and prices at all.[3] It is also interested in the competitive and chaotic processes through which value is produced such that certain geographical patterns inevitably result, such as the building up and letting rot (simultaneously) of capitalist landscapes. In this lineage it is less important to solve the transformation or reduction problem than to understand what it is about Marx's notion of value that raises these sorts of questions in the first place. As such, our interest in value cannot be decided on narrow problems alone. This leads easily, if not smoothly, to matters such as what other existing kinds of validated labor there are in capitalism, whether capitalism is something around which absolutely determinate boundaries can even be placed, forms of labor that are not validated and/or unwaged, and the like. I have been interested, in other words, in a more explicitly social-political idea of value, but one that as I have mentioned, does not reduce back to a theory of capital. (To Elson's credit, she draws out of Marx's value theory of labor certain qualities of labor that she argues would beset any mode of production: that labor would always have individual and social aspects, therefore responding to individual and social needs, as well as a concrete aspect identifiable by the different kinds of work that go on, and an abstract aspect, labor as energetic human activity per se. One can quibble over how to dissect this fourfold of labor and the boundaries of the different categories, but her reading still has a lot to recommend it: somehow the different qualities of transformative human activity, activity geared to the production of life, make themselves felt. The major difference I have with her conclusions concern what I have described as the value of the limit.)

Nor have I produced a reading of Marx that deeply engages his influences and the differences (or affinities) he has with them or a reading that offers a diagnosis of contemporary capitalism. Influences cannot be denied—from Aristotle, Spinoza, Kant, and Hegel to the long tradition of political economy whose nomenclature Marx gamely and enthusiastically accepts, if only to undermine. There is a huge amount to learn from writers such as Chris Arthur, who provides a superbly rigorous Hegelian reading of *Capital*, or Louis Althusser and Étienne Balibar, whose Spinozan rereading of the same book absolutely refuses the Hegelian influence on the later Marx. One can add Kojin Karatani's Kantian reading and alternative takes on the Hegelian, per Vinay Gidwani, and on the Spinozan, per Gilles Deleuze and Félix Guattari, Michael Hardt and Antonio Negri, and Cesare Casarino.[4] Reading Marx as the site of an engagement with other thinkers and writers is essential work, but it is not the route chosen here, which opts to follow how, in a manner of speaking, Marx performs concepts of value at the level of his texts. If it seems that I have thereby cut him off at the root, I hope to compensate at least somewhat by drilling down in a less familiar way and producing findings that are of interest.

There is no contesting that Marx has a keen interest in accurately capturing the real social processes shaping the capitalist world that is rapidly gaining ground in his day. At the end of the day, this is what many readers want, a Marx who clarifies the reality under which the citizens (or not, as the case may be) of capitalism labor and what needs to be done to make the world different. It is also inherent in some of the work just named. For example, Arthur and Althusser, the Hegelian and the anti-Hegelian, each would agree with that intent (although very differently and for separate reasons). The idea of a *primarily* social-scientific Marx—that is, a Marx who offers an objective, albeit politically committed, perspective on reality[5]—is a special interest of interpreters such as David Harvey, for whom Marx's explanations of how capitalism actually operates in the real world have always been paramount, whether considering his first major reading of Marx, *The Limits to Capital*, or the more recent, *Companion to Marx's "Capital."* I think it is fair to say that for Harvey the Hegelian Marx or the Spinozan Marx plays second fiddle to the Marx who seeks insight into the harsh realities of class exploitation, economic unruliness, and the power of commodities to distort human desire and alienate us from the very world we are making. It is no surprise that these social-scientific versions account for an enormous part of the interest in Marx, including the occasional concessionary statement by the mass media that Marx is rather perspicacious about the turbulent effects and dynamics of capitalism. Not surprisingly, these mass media do rather less with the politically radical side of Marx's social science, its normative (I will not say teleological) stance on the *nonnecessity* (ultimately) of capitalism.

Despite the convincingness of any of these interpretations, though, there is no substitute for reading Marx for oneself. Every honest interpreter of Marx and each of the writers I identify would say as much, and this ultimately also is the ground for this book. When I read Marx's writings, what I find is that my understanding is altered upon repeat readings and that any one systematic reading (Hegelian, Spinozan, etc.) forces one to overlook something of interest that Marx might also be saying. What I have come to think is that it is not simply that no interpretation is exhaustive. This is common sense these days; no one is to have the last word, and many can be partly right. It instead is that Marx wrote a great deal and did not always interpret and deploy his concepts in the same ways. It is possible of course to speak of a difference between an immature Marx and a mature Marx or of an epistemological break between an early and a late Marx.[6] That is not what I mean. I mean that there is more dispersion of ideas and gaps between them, more of their multiplicity and blooming and careening within the same textual moments than many might want to admit. This seems to me to warrant some extended treatment. I have chosen then to read Marx as freshly as possible (though this is not a naïve reading), to not forsake the seemingly stray analysis or off-the-cuff comment about value, and to be attentive to what happens on the outskirts. The works of Marx I contend with, therefore, I see *here* not as the result of their influences, including departures from them, and not as the result of Marx's own objective of critically anatomizing the capitalism of his day and, by extension, ours but rather as the modalities of value whose plurality is their own result. This I find, as I sketch out at the end of the book, lends itself to furthering the value-laden political imaginaries that getting beyond capitalism but remaining outside utopian longings require.

I now offer a few words about the texts I focus on and what is salient about their particular moments. If I briefly repeat certain elements of the preceding argument, I do so by way of an overview of which texts have informed my readings. The first thing to say is that I stick by and large to texts that are widely read and easily obtainable in any form, whether in print or electronically. Volume 1 of *Capital*, part 1 especially, in which Marx introduces the idea of value without yet proceeding to the idea of capital, is where I begin. There is a lot worth pondering in the separation of and space between the two ideas and, equally, in Marx's choice to introduce the notion of value beforehand. It is true that he held that the concept of value leads to the concept of capital, but this is not the same as saying there is a nonstop flight between the two or that they are reducible to each other, as is often suggested, tacitly or otherwise, in the literatures pertaining to Marx and Marxism. On the contrary, as Fredric Jameson recently notes, Marx holds these mutually attracting poles apart with great energy, though also with a bit more punch than Jameson allows.[7] Whereas Jameson laments that part 1 really is a "complete treatise in its own right" (13), with its own separate climactic moments that "block the reading of the rest of *Capital* itself" (46), I see Marx already at work positing value's differences in different modes of production (the passages are well known; I treat them in chapter 1) and thus describing a frame for the value–capital couplet that does not reduce value to capital. Jameson's "block" therefore marks in my reading the vitality to which I refer earlier or, as Althusser might put it, marks the success of Marx's failure, the symptom of a broader sensibility at work. But it also is a mark of the virtual dimension that value might be said to occupy, and that is value–capital's shaky ground. I am equally taken with and turn next to "The Chapter on Money" in Marx's *Grundrisse*. Of particular interest is that the idea of value is suspended, so to speak, within Marx's analysis of so-called labor money, or time chits, a proposal floated by certain utopian socialists of Marx's time (and earlier). How Marx addresses the manner by which their schemes fail in the goal to make value manifest runs in parallel to his own ideas concerning the failure of value to manifest in the commodity society and capital. More than this, Marx seems to suspend value above the reach of any commodity-based form of production, to keep it within the play of problem/solution, and, as I read across the "lives" of value, to posit an existence for value that ever is only in versions of its own incompleteness.

There are numerous places in the third volume of *Capital* where something of special interest also occurs. Marx simply interrupts his line of argument to posit the difference that associated production or associated labor would make to value relations. These interruptions within the text of *Capital*, perhaps paralleling Vinay Gidwani's notion of "capital [the social formation] interrupted," are quite jarring, seeming to come out of nowhere, but often full of excitement.[8] These narrative breaks have the effect of altering what cartographers and designers call the figure–ground relation. In the well-drafted relation, edges are drawn in such a way as to show what to perceive as foreground and what to perceive as background. It is the opposite where figure–ground relations are unclear. But a good drawing can just as easily intend to disrupt, to beg the question of figure and ground. Gestalt diagrams are a good example: Is that a drawing of two vases side by side or two silhouetted faces looking at each other? Is that an elderly woman or a rabbit? These metaphors are good for what happens in Marx's narrative break. Where the notion of value comes from, what impulses give rise to it, what desires it is a part of, and what "continents" it rightly belong in are all called into question in these interesting moments of the (never-finished) third volume of *Capital*. (Examples may be found in the other volumes of *Capital*, too. But I will draw from volume 3.) I may be saying enough for certain alarms to go off concerning whether I endorse or, worse, intend to resurrect the old argument that Marx intends value, as abstract labor or socially necessary labor time, to be perfectible after capitalism, under socialism or communism. That is, does Marx mean that value, perfected by capitalism, will be perfected even further by what is to come next and that all that is required for centralized planning of production is to appropriate the means of production and get the value formula (the production and distribution of labor time and use values) right? This question has been at the center of controversy for a very long time. That the answer could be yes has been refuted soundly and vigorously. I take no issue with that refutation. It is a problem, though, that in the process of refutation, a conflation between value and capital occurs.[9] I think this conflation is not at all necessary and indeed makes it difficult to see some of the important tensions that lurk in Marx's value tropes. Value does not reduce to the deus ex machina of capitalism; getting rid of capitalism does not mean getting rid of value. By the same token, not getting rid of value does not mean instantiating a corrected capitalism.

To the extent that a huge problem of capitalism is the imbalances it inflicts onto social life, I resist, in the final parts of the book, the idea that a better mode of production (call it associated production) would get rid of imbalances, bringing life and work, means of production and forces of production, and necessities and surpluses into balance with each other. Here is where the provocation of Greek art that I broach earlier enters, pulling with it in train Marx's continuing fascination with "things." Such a provocation, really an experimental reading that runs against the grain of how Marx is usually received, depends upon pitting Marx's pluralized system of value against itself (which is to say, for itself!). The provocation is relevant insofar as a good deal of the current search for alternative value systems seems to place a premium on social coherence, a suitable, nonexploitative *fitness* among diverse social practices. The anthropologist David Graeber defines, for example, value as the way in which individual actions become socially meaningful.[10] Without rejecting this idea outright, because it does comport with a certain conception of value, I find reason to inject a stream of value thinking to a different purpose: the search for disjunction, for the out of joint, for a principle of destabilization of meaning (but not so far as to wreak havoc). But I argue all of this out in due course.

This book does not, therefore, test whether Marx is right about capitalism and its actual shape on the ground. I have elsewhere had such an interest, and I still do. Here, I largely accept what Marx has to say and see my job as investigating what he expresses by way of a social and political imaginary that continually kicks the can of value down the road in ways that I think are intriguing, irrepressible, indispensable, and not a little unpredictable. Notably, Marx does not master the lives of value. Value theory in that singular sense often given it, as a theory of capital, remains his unfinished project but, I think, also obscures a larger project. Instead, he scatters the lives of value (I do not say by grand design or with a sense of contentment) across multiple texts and fragments of text. They comprise a *lumpenproletariat* of statements, ideas, images, and speculative impression that are worth tarrying with. Value is not self-evident. It calls out for rediscovery and reinvention, and that is why I have written this book.

Part I

1

The Value–Capital Couplet and How to Break It

A Terrain of Agreement?

How odd that value, the great compass by which nearly everything in Marx's political economy can be found—commodity, capital, labor, etc., etc., etc.—eludes easy use. No sooner does the needle point north to capitalism as the treacherous land ahead than north *moves*; the needle spins and points to other lands—utopian socialism, associated production, and some other et ceteras Marx gets to in the first chapters of *Capital*. It is not that any of these lands might be the one true north which causes value's way-finding abilities to shift. It is that Marx himself is this north, and he won't stand still. He (and what he wants value to explain and to find out) is the one circling the compass, exerting the magnetic attraction, pulling value's needle around. Marx himself might not be fully aware of his own influence. But he exerts it all the same. Reading value is inevitably an interpretive act. Does value not serve as guide to virtually everything that is wrong about capitalism, everything that is in need of negation? But might it also be the guide to everything that is right about associated production, everything that needs positing? Or might the compass be most useful if the needle kept quaking just a little, forcing its users to cut their own trail? Yes, yes, and yes. The end result is that value needs to be understood as much by what happens to it when it is put to work as by the work we think it is going to do.

There are, then, two truths that Marx's readers immediately

confront, most especially when they start with *Capital*. To read Marx and *not get* value is to have been asleep. And value is very difficult to think.[1] What has nonetheless emerged is what could be regarded as a broad terrain of agreement, which I eventually show to be a slice of value's horizon. This terrain includes an agreement as to what value is for Marx (an agreement that concerns the coupling of value and capital) and why from within this agreement value is difficult to think. If there is a general point that a wide range of Marx's readers might converge upon, perhaps it is that in a capitalist society value must appear as other than what it is. Not only does it not stalk about with a label on its forehead, to use Marx's expression, but it requires forms other than itself to stalk about at all. Why is value displaced and dispersed in this way? Very quickly, leaping over a great number of nuances and exceptions, here is the chain of reasoning. A capitalist society primarily is a commodity-producing society. (Or if one's eye is on the diversity of productive activity in society, the commodity-producing activities are the sine qua non of the society's capitalist aspect.) That is to say, social wealth in capitalist societies primarily takes the form of commodities. A commodity producer, as we all know—or as we all know Marx says—makes commodities primarily to sell them on the market in exchange for a different commodity that some other commodity producer has made. On these terms, a commodity's value is capable of being expressed only in terms of another, different commodity. It makes little sense to say a pair of shoes is worth that same pair of shoes, that in other words, it is worth itself. As a consumer or end user, I might in fact feel this way about my own pair of shoes. They are worth having because they protect my feet or look good with my faded jeans or both. The shoemaker or the owner of the shoe factory may feel this way, too, about the shoes she or he makes. The shoes are worth making because they appear to be a source of success, pride, etc. But all of that is different from the shoes' value as commodities produced for the market. In the market context, such and such a number of shoes is worth such and such an amount of some other commodity that the shoemaker can purchase after the sale of the shoes (or beforehand, with credit), perhaps a car to get back and forth to work or raw materials to make more shoes with. Either way, the value of one commodity can be expressed only by a different commodity. As Marx draws this idea out across an increasing number of examples of goods produced for the market—linen, coats, bibles, wheat, iron, and so on—it is soon apparent that exchange is smoothened when a single commodity serves as the medium of exchange for all the others. Then, soon comes money and its forms: gold and silver coins, paper bills, bank notes, credit, and so on. The value of one commodity, of any and every commodity, can be expressed in the form of money, money being the universal equivalent. When it is asked what exactly is being expressed when commodities are exchanged on the market, readers of Marx know the answer: human labor in the abstract. For Marx labor is the common element of almost every kind of commodity, and when different commodities exchange with each other, although *only in the act* of exchange, the different kinds of labor used to make them (whether shoemaking or automobile assembly) are irrelevant. Labor *in the abstract* is the common element, and the measure of this labor in the abstract is time. Such and such a number of shoes are equivalent to such and such a number of cars because each has taken such and such an average number of hours of human labor to make. Value in a capitalist society simply is, at first blush, the abstract human labor that goes into making that society's commodities. The value of any one commodity is the portion of total abstract human labor represented by that commodity *insofar as* it exchanges for another commodity. The mechanism developed to handle the totality of exchanges and to be the bearer of value is money and, thus, price. Therefore, commodity value takes the form of money, expressed in price.

Hence, a key point is that value takes a form other than what it is. (Even those who argue that capitalism tends toward or has even reached a state in which labor time ceases to be the measure of value—because, for example, work is increasingly performed by nonhuman machines or because the knowledge economy renders time a poor measure of value—would agree that Marx's concept of value is such that value appears as other.) But why must labor be expressed as value? Why must labor appear as other than what it is? This obvious question also produces an answer that I think most of Marx's readers would agree upon. Briefly, the reasoning is as follows: Something about commodity exchange necessitates that labor appear in the form of value. As explained, Marx argues that when producers of two different commodities exchange them, it must be because of something these commodities have in common. It cannot be the material properties of the commodities themselves, and it cannot be the specific, concrete labor necessary to make a particular commodity, since these different concrete labors are caught up in these commodities' material differences that have already been ruled out. It can be only labor in the abstract that is the common element. Marx adds that this process of abstracting is not something about which the producers are even aware; it is just a consequence of commodity exchange. Labor appears in the form of value as a result of the market. But there are essential points to add. Producing commodities on a competitive basis yields an average amount of labor time that is specific to each kind of commodity, an average that commodity producers must keep up with or, ideally, reduce. And because value is indexed to present, ongoing fluctuations of average labor time, it is highly destabilizing to existing commodities. A commodity's value at the time of its production—for example, the value of the equipment used to produce automobiles—does not belong to it in perpetuity but can rise or fall throughout the period of its use. Thus, when it comes round to considering how a capitalist, value-inscribed economy reproduces itself over the course of years, it is no surprise to find that it does so in a highly chaotic fashion. What something is worth today does not guarantee its position tomorrow. Not the least of the subsequent disturbances are the bouts of unemployment, redundancies, and layoffs—not to mention the rise of part-time work, casual employment, contract labor, multiple-earner households, and so on—that go along with the competitive drive to reduce labor time. (This peculiar illogic of capitalism is, Marx once wrote, the best reason to be done with the whole system.)

The most significant point Marx makes concerning why labor

must take the form of value brings us back to money and its role. The availability of money and its function of circulating throughout society is neither what gives commodities their value nor what enables them to have price. Marx sees it the other way around. Money can serve to express value because it is *already* predicated on value relations. Money is a commodity among other commodities and is merely, if crucially, singled out for the purpose of being the universal equivalent. This has incredibly important implications. It means we can and, indeed, ought to posit the question of what happens when the money commodity is brought to the market with the intention of getting more money back, without violating the rule of equivalence that commodities are supposed to be exchanged with each other on the basis of equal value. Again, it is known how Marx solves the problem: a commodity for sale exists that has the property of generating more value than it has itself. That commodity is labor power, and the site where its peculiar property is evident is in commodity production, not the sphere of circulation (the market). In capitalism, therefore, it is not simply that labor takes the form of value. This labor needs to be wage labor (i.e., labor power must be commodified and put to the task of creating more value than it has itself). Capitalism must be a class-based system in which the surplus value produced is up for appropriation.

We have now moved beyond our starting point. Value appears in a form other than itself and (a second point of broad agreement) masks the form that is crucial to its appearance, wage labor (or its analogues, piecework and salary work) as the source of surplus value. Value masks and is masked. It not only is displaced to a form other than itself but is a process that displaces and veils other things, relegating them to the sphere of the noneconomic (the formation of classes, the coming to be of wage labor). This probably is the other central point upon which most readers of Marx would agree when it comes to value.

Looking out from this terrain of agreement, I think several related truths appear that tend to structure readings of Marx's political economy. First is that value and capital belong together in a mutually exhaustive way: capital is the highest expression of value such that the end of value would be the end of capital. Second, value concerns the question of balance, equity, equilibrium. It becomes the name for a process that allows Marx to hypothesize and sometimes observe what happens when commodity production and exchange across society or between specific sectors falls out of balance and efforts are made to put things right, to set value-creating processes back on their feet. Third, when Marx is taken to task for what he misses or overstates, his notion of value is taken pretty much in these terms, if only to complicate it, supplement it, or even dethrone it. That is to say, I think very few readers would insist that Marx does *not* say what I have tried to summarize, even as they devise new flight lines. There are plentiful interpretations of what it means that value takes a form other than itself, thus being unable to appear on its own terms; what it means that value masks the forms it takes as being value laden, thus actively intervening in the shaping of social action; or given the enormous tension between the historical aspects of Marx's depiction and its seemingly more strictly logical aspects,[2] what it means that actual capitalist formations are, as Gibson-Graham insists, infinitely more complex than the sketch implies, thus necessitating study of a wide range of productive activities and logics and the question of whether indeed these all knit together into a seamless landscape of value.[3] Conversely, interpretations can go the other way, too, as when value, reimagined, becomes a way to resolve some of the tensions that have erupted between different politically radical stances.[4] All of this is true. Nonetheless, it seems to me that this sketch is what readers of Marx would include in a précis on value if asked to draw up one.

Value without Capital

The preceding brief on value has at least one chink in its armor. In the first volume of *Capital*, from which the brief is drawn, Marx describes what value is and what sort of labor expresses itself in value terms (abstract labor) and then proceeds to his famous analysis of the commodity fetish, read by so many as a screed against our disregard of the labor content of the commodity (about which more in a moment), *before* he broaches the subjects of wage labor, exploitation, surplus value, and, indeed, capital. Some interpreters are troubled by this. Isn't it a violation of the value concept that there is no explanation of the labor discipline necessary to reproduce the wage form and thus to ensure the abstraction of labor?[5] Isn't it premature to go on about the commodity fetish *before* letting on that something untoward happens in commodity production behind the factory gates? On both counts it could be yes, but this is not a required route. On the contrary, I propose accepting this fissure between value and capital in the first part of *Capital* so as to find therein the first signs that value has a broader remit. In plain terms, at this juncture in the text the concept of capital is not necessary to round out what Marx is doing with value, since he is up to something else.

The pivotal moment is Marx's development of the commodity fetish, an understanding of which is helped by drawing upon certain elements of the value sketch I just laid out. "Exchange value," Marx writes, is "the necessary mode of expression, or form of appearance, of value," the only form in which the value of commodities can become manifest (128). Why? We already know. The value of linen, to take an example, cannot be expressed in linen—value "can only appear in the social relation between commodity and commodity" (139). Labor in the abstract, as the common element in commodity production, can appear only in the exchange of commodities, since abstraction is a facet of market exchange. But because Marx is dealing with a set of dependent, displaced relations, value-creating labor can become value only "in its congealed state, in objective form"— that is, embodied in the form of some object (142). Put these objects into an exchange relation, and they become, as it were, value for each other. Marx here encourages us to grasp the peculiarities of the matter. If every commodity "must be related to another commodity as equivalent, and therefore must make the physical shape of another commodity into its own value-form," then use value becomes the form for value to manifest (148). This is the first peculiarity, which if so, implies a second, that concrete labor is the form for the manifestation of abstract labor. These build to a third peculiarity, that individual "private labor takes the form of its opposite, namely labor in its directly social form" (151). These ideas are very well laid out by the time Marx introduces the commodity fetish. We understand that there is an odd play of contrasts in the commodity society, that somehow thousands or millions of private individuals and private acts are supposed to face each other and thus come to have social content, and that acts of market exchange turn private labor into social labor by distributing use values to those who pay for them. All of this is apparent before the commodity fetish appears. What then *is* the commodity fetish? And what is Marx trying to say with it?

Commodity Fetish: First Cut

Contrary to a lot of assumptions concerning what Marx means by the commodity fetish, he does not seem to mean that behind the exchange of commodities, there is an inscrutable secret: abstract labor. He writes that for anyone who cares to really think about commodity production and exchange, abstract labor—value—is reasonably obvious. He does state, though, that we are not aware of abstract labor.[6] This seems like a contradiction, for if abstract labor is no lasting secret, then why aren't we aware of it? I think the answer simply might be that we do not need to be aware of it. The significance of the commodity fetish is that our knowledge of it does not make it go away. We can study labor relations; we can analyze the conditions of labor; we can come to appreciate labor and working people; we can trace the commodity chains and the labors that are behind them. We can read Marx's *Capital*. But the fetish is neither a psychological nor a perceptual issue to resolve, nor even an analytical issue, really. It in some sense describes the limits of knowledge as a critical, social power. The commodity fetish is, Marx writes, "inseparable from the production of commodities" (165).

This means that our knowledge of the commodity fetish is not to be used to develop a plan *on the basis of commodity production and money* for balanced distribution of labor times within the social division of labor or for fair wages and shared profits: in doing so we would still be in the field of the fetish. Knowledge of the fetish has the power neither to negate existing society nor to constitute the society to come. It tells us only about the necessary consequences of our actions as commodity producers and exchangers. When Marx writes that relations between persons really have become social relations between things, we might translate that as we let our things do our thinking for us rather than thinking for ourselves directly. The possibility of effective thought is displaced onto and forfeited to things; it appears in them, not us. This does not mean thought has no role at all. We think about how exchanging things can maximize exchange value, on the one hand, and we think about how things are of use value to us, on the other. And it appears that a lot of social reproduction gets done on those strategic thought bases alone, as it indeed must, since, again, the market in things mediates social relations between producers. But the fact that private labor in the commodity society actually has a social character does not need to announce itself, precisely because it already appears in the form of money and in the fact of commodity (thingly) exchange, instead.

Marx makes a curious statement while discussing the commodity fetish, positing that "reflection on the forms of human life," even scientific reflection, "takes a course directly opposite to their real development," historically (168). As an instance, he contemplates the usual course of reflection on the commodity society as performed by his predecessors and contemporaries *and* as performed by himself. He begins:

> The forms which stamp products as commodities, and
> which are therefore the preliminary requirements for the
> circulation of commodities, already possess the fixed
> quality of natural forms of social life before man seeks
> to give an account, not of their historical character, for
> in his eyes they are immutable, but of their content and
> meaning. Consequently, it was solely the analysis of
> the prices of commodities which led to the determina-
> tion of the magnitude of value, and solely the common
> expression of all commodities in money which led to

the establishment of their character as values. It is
however precisely this finished form of the world of
commodities—the money form—which conceals the
social character of private labor and the social relations between the individual workers, by making those
relations appear as relations between material objects,
instead of revealing them plainly. (168–69)

What Marx is saying here is that the normal analytical course,
one he does not really yet dispute, is to try to work backward
from the commodity form itself in order to understand what it
means and what it entails. Both he and bourgeois economics, he
states, work on the basis of phenomenal forms to see what in-
sights they can gain. But no degree of closeness to phenomenal
forms will get these forms to speak their truth in and of themselves. Marx then seems to straightforwardly confess that he
is caught in the same predicament as the political economists.

If I state that coats or boots stand in a relation to linen
because the latter is the universal incarnation of abstract
human labor, the absurdity of the statement is self-
evident. Nevertheless, when the producers of coats and
boots bring these commodities into a relation with linen,
or with gold or silver (and this makes no difference
here), as the universal equivalent, the relation between
their own private labor and the collective labor of society appears to them in exactly this absurd form. (169)

Marx himself has no special power to make things speak. He
sees that his own speech, alluding back to his elaboration of the
forms of value in preceding sections of chapter 1—namely, that
coats, boots, or *any* nonlinen commodity can be traded for linen
because of their common basis in labor and because one type of
commodity stands apart from the rest to serve as the equivalent
and mediate exchange—is as absurd as the statement made by
commodity producers when they use money to speak to each
other. Both the concept (Marx's) and the practice (the producers') are absurd. This is interesting. Marx is not saying that his

statement is made out to be absurd by those who don't catch his brilliance: it is self-evidently absurd. Why? No matter what, the nature of a commodity does not announce itself on its surface. Marx touches, so to speak, the commodity with his concept; producers touch money every day. But no matter who speaks for the commodity, an element of absurdity in that speech is unavoidable; no matter who touches it physically in exchange or engages in price comparisons, the absurdity of the situation is there. The absurdity is that abstract labor can be thought about or not thought about. Awareness or dim awareness does not change a thing. Commodities do not need us to think about the abstraction of labor that they entail. They do not need us to consider the social character of the producers' private labor.

What I am saying is that although Marx is, in part, commenting on the science of political economy (his contemporaries' and predecessors') and on how much they are able to get right and wrong on the basis of appearances, he also is commenting on the nature of the proof he himself is offering. *The opacity of the commodity infects and becomes part of his own speech.* Marx ends these particular thoughts by writing that "the categories of bourgeois economics consist precisely of forms of this kind. They are forms of thought which are socially valid, and therefore objective, for the relations of production belonging to this historically determined mode of social production, i.e., commodity production" (169). But after almost one hundred pages, how far has Marx himself been able to clear an enlightened path? He does not want to express "with social validity" the conditions of the commodity society, and yet his analysis of commodity society seems close to being caught within those very conditions. But the absurdity that trumps all is still that in spite of the absurdity of the manner in which social labor appears (or precisely because of this), modern society can be founded on a rock of silence. Don't forget that we can of course actually surmise the process of labor abstraction that takes place—Marx does not think the truth is difficult to divine—but the commodity is such that we do not need to. The irony of the situation should be fully apparent. We live in a society that does not require its own truth to be known. Marx's words are, thus, like things circulating among other things, changing nothing unless "things change." There even is the intimation that the deeper the critique of the fetish goes, the greater the intensification of the fetish, of the absurdity of the situation in which we find ourselves. Such absurdity then seems likely to become the source of its own pleasures, as David Clarke indicates when writing of the possibilities of a rapprochement between Marx's commodity fetishism and psychoanalysis. The commodity in some sense mocks us. What else could it embody but social labor? What else could happen in the commodity society except that prior access to social labor be withheld? Under these conditions it would seem only one kind of victory exists for those in the know (though Marx strains against it): "a certain pleasure is attendant on maintaining a belief that the subject is nonetheless aware is fictive."[7] We know that commodity production abstracts human labor but invest the commodity anyway with extra powers. Precisely because it is possible to be silent about social labor, it is possible to fill it up with pleasure of an ironic sort or, indeed, pleasures that are far less canny. For only "perverted consciousness," as Zygmunt Bauman puts it, imagines that "man can change his plight merely by acquiring the right consciousness," even of the "murkier aspects of his condition."[8]

Where do things stand, then? There are two observations to make. The first is just that the commodity form of social life does not need a social plan. Second, if we ask why, it is because we allow the continual market traffic in things to take precedence. Abstraction of labor is not socially planned; it is at once an effect of commodity exchange and a precondition for that exchange. This is what Marx is getting at in the idea of the commodity fetish. I conclude the first cut at the commodity fetish by stating that Marx uses the fetish idea to repeat much of what he has already said only to underscore again the opacity of the commodity, not so much to our knowledge as to its capacity to change itself. In a world that is mediated by things, we cannot depend on things, the manipulation of things, to change that world. Disclosure of the operations of the commodity fetish has the power neither to negate existing society nor to constitute the society to come. It tells us only about the necessary consequences of market interactions, our interactions, when we cede and reify the terrain of the social.

By now we should understand (without the aid of the concepts of surplus value and wage labor) that Marx thinks that if private individuals conducted their affairs in such a way that the sociality of their existence were mediated indirectly by something (the market) over which they had no control, wouldn't it be better if they planned their sociality, arranged for it directly? Consider that value as a process occurs when during exchange the intrinsically *social* character of the *private* labor that produces commodities is itself produced. The social character can be revealed through analysis and thought, but it does not need to be. What is more and maybe worse is that since commodity exchange is considered accidental by Marx (and subject to all sorts of vagaries, which I get to in the following section), the social-character potential of private labor may remain just that, a potential. What possibly is even weirder is that this value process is retroactive: value is only value once exchange occurs. So the real relations among persons not only takes the form of things but also are accidental and only retroactive. Who would want to live in such conditions? and, Don't you, the members of an ostensibly free and equal society, want better? would seem to be the questions to ask ourselves (and this despite the scarred experience of centralized planning).[9] Embedded in Marx's analysis of the commodity fetish is the idea that value not simply is descriptive but points to what must be done by those who would go beyond the commodity society. They must consciously rather than incidentally or accidentally construct their society. At the very beginning of section 4 of chapter 1, the section in which the fetish is introduced, Marx notes that "in all situations, the labor-time it costs to produce the means of subsistence must necessarily concern mankind, although not to the same degree at different stages of development" (164). This statement is part and parcel of his argument that the determinants of value are not the source of the commodity fetish. The source of the commodity fetish is the imposition of the commodity thing itself.[10]

Commodity Fetish: Second Cut

In the section on the fetish and, indeed, elsewhere in the first part of *Capital*, Marx notes that one of the problems with his forerunners and certain of his contemporaries is that so many of them consider the commodity society to be the result of natural drives and natural human attributes, a society without a history. It is in consideration of this that Marx offers what I call a second cut at understanding the commodity fetish and its perpetuation. In this second cut Marx offers another sort of proof of its and value's existence. And this proof is geared not to commodities and ultimately capital but to the abolition of the commodity society.

Continuing straight on from the passage on the absurd that I use in the previous section, Marx writes that the secret of value (though we have seen he does not really think it is much of a secret at all) "vanishes . . . as soon as we come to other forms of production" (169). This begins a very well-known sequence in which Marx contrasts such a variety of forms: Robinson Crusoe alone on his island, a feudal estate, a peasant household, communism, and, finally, the commodity society again (169–73). It seems that in every form, save that of the commodity society, the social relations that bind the society are social relations in full evidence and are ones that the members need to know about. (Obviously, this is not grounds for endorsing all of these forms. That social relations appear along with the products people make is a necessary but insufficient ground for endorsement. The difference is one of real equality and freedom.) The following passage on communism is worth reproducing in full:

> Let us finally imagine, for a change, an association of free men, working with the means of production held in common, and expending their many different forms of labor-power in full self-awareness as one single social labor force. All the characteristics of Robinson's labor are repeated here, but with the difference that they are social instead of individual. All Robinson's products were exclusively the result of his own personal labor

and they were therefore directly objects of utility for him personally. The total product of our imagined association is a social product. One part of this product serves as fresh means of production and remains social. But another part is consumed by the members of the association as means of subsistence. This part must therefore be divided amongst them. The way this division is made will vary with the particular kind of social organization of production and the corresponding level of social development attained by the producers. We shall assume, but only for the sake of a parallel with the production of commodities, that the share of each individual producer in the means of subsistence is determined by his labor-time. Labor-time would in that case play a double part. Its apportionment in accordance with a definite social plan maintains the correct proportion between the different functions of labor and the various needs of the associations. On the other hand, labor-time also serves as a measure of the part taken by each individual in the common labor, and of his share in the part of the total product destined for individual consumption. The social relations of the individual producers, both towards their labor and the products of their labor, are here transparent in their simplicity, in production as well as in distribution. (171–72)

What is accomplished by the whole of the comparative sequence (to which readers will have to refer themselves), which includes this picture of a community of free individuals? Marx has shown the possibility of nonfetishizing social forms and, thus, the historical peculiarity of the commodity fetish. More important, he has shown—*in value terms*—the possibility of alternatives to the commodity society. He has taken what he has made so familiar about the commodity and radically rewritten that story while retaining a familiarity with value, which he establishes by anatomizing the commodity in the first place. He does not so much radically break with value theory as he displaces it and describes it in a sort of perfected form that makes a break with the commodity. This is significant for a certain way of reading Marx as someone for whom value and capital are said ultimately to form an unbreakable bond.

And yet there is still more going on here. Marx notes the value comparison between communistic and commodity production is drawn "for the sake of a parallel." We can read this to mean that communism would work differently from what Marx describes; he means only to give us some idea of how it might work in terms that are familiar to his readers. In other words, we should not allow this comparison with commodity production to give us a diminished and impoverished sense of communism. That is the important reading offered by those careful to say that communism does not reduce to an economy of labor times.[11] But this reading may be nudged further along by positing that the parallel also works the other way around. Marx's parallel shows how diminished and impoverished commodity society is when contrasted with *value in the "association of free men."* These are not just different ways of saying the same thing. As I argue in the next set of discussions, Marx shows, in an important sense, that value does not actually take place in capitalism. Value would then seem to occupy a very curious position. On the one hand, there is not an identity between a perfected value and communism. On the other hand, as I hope to show, there also is not an identity between value and the commodity society. This means that drawing a comparison among different modes of production by means of the value concept isn't just "for the sake of parallel"—or for the sake of a "parable," as Althusser writes of the role of the commodity fetish in Marx's analysis of value.[12] Value somehow *is* parallel, seeming to be neither the truth of commodity production and exchange nor adequate to properly formulate the community of free individuals. In other words, along with value thinkers such as Noel Castree and Gayatri Spivak, we might at this juncture consider value as an inscription without a clear referent, a tool that in some sense *invokes its own* devices upon which to work (despite the conflation each of these writers makes between value and capital).[13] We must consider, through to the end of this book, what to make of such a conundrum and, if possible, turn it into a value.

Does Value Exist?

In what sense does value eke out a threadbare existence in the commodity society? In what sense might it have no existence? These questions can be explored via Marx's analysis of money in the first part of *Capital* (i.e., during the before of surplus value, capital, and wage labor). Money is the essential crossroad at this stage because it is the most potent bearer of value, being at first blush capable of representing (being exchangeable for) all commodities and thus of liberating each commodity from its own value form. What Marx argues, though, is that it becomes impossible for money to actually succeed at being the preeminent value form, no matter if it is in circulation and ostensibly doing its job or if protected from the chaos and noise of circulation by being held as a hoard or in reserve.

The chains of liberty are forged as follows: Once gold or silver become "the direct incarnation of all human labor," Marx writes, "men are henceforth related to each other in their process of production in a purely atomistic way"—individualistically, privately. "Their own relations of production therefore assume a material shape which is independent of their control and their conscious individual action. This situation is manifested first by the fact that the products of men's labor universally take on the form of commodities" (187). Commodities and the exchange of commodities are, in other words, the only ways these private acts of production *could* be related to each other. "The riddle of the money fetish"—that it can and must stand for an infinity of dissimilar use values—"is therefore the riddle of the commodity fetish, now become visible and dazzling to our eyes" (187). Money, that is, can only represent value because the things (commodities) that it helps to circulate can already be represented to each other as values. But once this process is ongoing, the steps whereby commodities can be represented by money "vanishes in its own result, leaving no trace behind" (187). Again, it is not because of money that labor can be abstracted, for this abstraction is immanent to commodity exchange. This makes money the site of the following double riddle: (1) money depends on and reproduces those relations in which commodities, in exchange, are already values (188), which (2) can be ignored, or even never known, precisely because of money. The point, echoing the commodity fetish, is that money underscores not so much our forgetting of the origin of value but the nonnecessity of such knowledge. Money works by not needing to reveal the work it does. Or if you like, because it proves everything, money need not prove anything.

Yet in having shown how value can take the money form, Marx has set the stage for exposing as fallacy that this actually happens. This is demonstrated in multiple ways, the sum of which seems to indicate that value in the commodity society is, so to speak, "less than zero," a number eternally waiting to be counted. In chapter 3 of *Capital*, Marx investigates the relationship between money prices and the magnitude of value. The latter necessarily concerns the share held by a particular commodity of the "social labor time which is inherent in the process by which its value is created." In the ideal world with which Marx begins, commodities trade with each other on the basis of equivalent magnitudes of value, but necessarily expressed in price. But "with the transformation of the magnitude of value into the price," price being a manifestation of the market, "this necessary relation appears as the exchange ratio between a single commodity and the money commodity which exists outside it. This relation, however, may express both the magnitude of value of the commodity and the greater or lesser quantity of money for which it can be sold under the given circumstances" (196). The exact exchange ratio becomes, in other words, accidental, and it is inherent to the price form that prices and values can deviate from each other. "This is not a defect, but, on the contrary, it makes this form [price] the adequate one for a mode of production whose laws can only assert themselves as blindly operating averages between constant irregularities" (196). This is a somewhat difficult idea, but what it conveys is the reassertion that value cannot appear alone— something we knew already—and that even the existence of its form cannot accurately represent it. And yet precisely because of this gap, the price form functions where value does not, even while price is an erstwhile expression of value. The reasoning has gone thus: if the market is a necessary institution for private producers to demonstrate (silently) that their labor is actually social and if price is the mechanism that makes that institution work, then when the vagaries of the market show themselves, prices are free to deviate from the ostensible values they represent. Price ceases to represent value. Value ceases to be represented. (Once Marx introduces the idea of surplus value and capital, however, he returns to this matter of deviation of price from value, saying it's necessary to conceptually equate price and value so that a proper explanation of surplus value can be made, one that shows that the market is not the source of surplus value. But he also downplays the significance of the deviation problem, writing that in practice capitalists keep in mind average, longer-run prices. This seems to me, however, just another instance of the price form's "adequacy" in dealing with oscillating circumstances. Indeed, he notes that "average prices do not directly coincide with the values of commodities, as Adam Smith, Ricardo, and others believe" [269n24].)

As we continue to chase it down in successive pages the coherency of the value form keeps losing shape and runs through our fingers like so much sand. We learn that certain "things such as conscience, honor, etc." can have price but no value (197). Thus, the chain that starts with value taking on the independent form of prices extends to the price form developing a further independence arbitrarily linking itself to anything. We learn that unlike other commodities that must ultimately fall out of circulation and be consumed, money must remain in circulation (although see my discussion of hoards in the following section). This prompts Marx to raise, on behalf of the commodity society, the question of how much money is actually needed for circulation to occur (213). Stipulations abound, but they all hinge on the rate of circulation of commodities and the sum of the values of commodities in circulation. In other words, how many transactions are taking place and what is their cumulative worth at any moment? Of course, there is no authority in the world that can say with any certainty. Marx goes over in the usual detail the many possible permutations and notes with some surprise, though, that if the long term is considered, there is a certain stability in the amount of money present, only to add "the exception of the violent perturbations which arise periodically, either from crises in production and commerce, or, more rarely, from changes in the value of money itself" (219). We find, too, that money is (was?) a physical, erodible substance. Coins wear down as they circulate, implying the "latent possibility" of replacing them with some other material "by symbols which. would serve the function of coins"—paper, for example (223). But this would compel the state to regulate these symbols, ensure their worth, etc. (226). It seems not only that value forms fade like invisible ink but that they require extraeconomic players to write them back in. So if value relations, as commodity fetish, have become collectively solidified as this giant, imposing thing, with money as its most stolid standard-bearer, further interrogation has revealed this thing as increasingly less stolid and thinglike, as less reliable as a representative of value the more we rely upon it for exactly that purpose. Money, as the most important form of value, develops a logic that intrudes into value's being, even as value relations continually beget money. Value becomes unhomely in its own house.

That value does not work, in the very midst of being put to work, is introduced very early into part 1 of *Capital*, almost as soon as Marx begins to analyze exchange relations. "Exchange-value appears first of all as the quantitative relation, the proportion, in which use-values of one kind exchange for use-values of another kind," a relation that "*changes constantly with time and place*" (126; emphasis added). Recall that different values in use—use values—ostensibly are exchanged on the basis that each embodies an equivalent of average labor time (i.e., each is an equal magnitude of value). Giving the example of the effect of power looms on the exchange values of textiles, Marx notes that if "labor-time . . . changes with every variation in the productivity of labor" (130), then the magnitude of value expressed in a given yardage of cloth changes. Value, therefore, if it can only manifest as exchange value in the first place, is forced to chase after a constantly moving target, and vice versa. Clearly, this is profoundly disrupting. "The same change in productivity which increases the fruitfulness of labor, and therefore the amount of use-values produced by it, also brings about a reduction in the value of this increased total amount, if it cuts down the total amount of labor-time necessary to produce the use-values. The converse also holds" (137). Such labor efficiencies may appear to be pretty advantageous, but to Marx they actually mean that value and material wealth are regularly involved in a gut-wrenching antagonism. "Real changes in the magnitude of value are neither unequivocally nor exhaustively reflected in their relative expression, or, in other words, in the magnitude of the relative value. The relative value of a commodity [i.e., how much of it I am going to have to produce and sell in order to purchase X amount of a different commodity that I need] may vary, although its value remain constant . . . ," and on Marx goes through a dizzying array of possible fluctuations in the magnitudes of value, until "finally, simultaneous variations in the magnitude of value and in the relative expression of that magnitude do not by any means have to correspond at all points" (146). In other words, every commodity producer faces the prospect of whether to trouble with the magnitude of value of her commodity, in light of the fact that every producer she seeks to trade with is wondering the same. The kicker of course is that she, as an individual commodity producer, does not even decide how much value her commodity actually expresses or will express, since this is a determination of the social average of labor time, a moving quantity. Quantities of value "vary continually, independently of the will, foreknowledge and actions of the exchangers" (167). Place these quantities on the market, and it so happens that someone cannot sell enough of what they have produced and that someone else runs out too soon. In order to resolve such problems, commodities, as we saw, end up being sold at prices that do not reflect their magnitudes of value or not sold all, or production of a certain sort of commodity may simply cease. Indeed, the *kinds* of commodities that commodity producers make (i.e., the social division of labor) change "behind the backs of the producers" (201). As a result of products becoming outmoded or superfluous, their individual producers may be left out in the cold.[14] "Commodities are in love with money," Marx writes, but the " 'course of true love never did run smooth' " (202).

I have noted how Marx points out that the price form and the market are well adapted to the awkward perturbations of value-laden production. But the sense has grown that value is not so much played by a cast of roving representations (money, commodity X, commodity Y, etc.) as it is simply a stranded figure, reduced to a shadowy existence, a character on the stage without an actor to play its part. This shadow or ghostly existence of value—a modality appearing in several strains of value-theoretic Marxist literature[15]—can also be considered an effect of Marx's text, value-in-use by his own hand. So even when Marx writes in chapter 3 that he will leave aside all of these many problems of how value is to take form, that he will assume exchange *is* running smoothly (i.e., commodities are circulating and the market is successfully matching prices to values, thus indicating the more or less regulatory role that value plays in commodity distribution and the allocation of labor times), he simply cannot seem to prevent himself from continuing to note how value just fails miserably. For he marches impatiently straight toward an introduction to another circulatory problem, the disequilibrium of sales and purchases. "Nothing could be more foolish than the dogma that because every sale is a purchase, and every purchase a sale, the circulation of commodities necessarily implies an equilibrium between sales and purchases" (208). This disequilibrium results in blockages to the flow of commodities and money such that circulation ultimately "bursts through all the temporal, spatial, and personal boundaries imposed by the direct exchange of products [barter]" (209). Indeed, Marx earlier notes that money is really posited when the exchange of goods is not working right; it emerges with the problem of the ever-widening (spatially, temporally, materially) circle of exchanges and contributes to that problem (182). Therefore, even in the form of circulation that preoccupies Marx for the entirety of part 1 of *Capital*, simple commodity circulation (i.e., C . . . M . . . C), crises are immanent because of the antithesis present in the commodity: it must at some point exchange the form of its value for that of another commodity, but it does not necessarily have to experience that change right away. Marx saves deeper discussion of crises until later and so is content for now to simply pose their immanence. But in some sense the damage is done; value sits like a dead letter.

What's So Wrong with the Commodity Society Anyway?

These points come to a head, I think, in Marx's discussion of hoards. The ultimate aim of the discussion is, we might surmise, to beg the question of accumulations of money that will begin to circulate as capital—M . . . C . . . M′—a frame within which to spy the dark inscape of surplus value. This is to short change the analysis of hoards, though. To very interesting effect, Marx uses the hoard to keep chipping away at simple circulation, sculpting every last analytical point he can, so perfecting the burdens to be passed along to the model of capital in later chapters—in whose pages capital will thus already have failed at value.

Marx writes that hoards, while historically present in many societies, are made possible in the commodity society through the interruption of simple circulation, as when commodity sales, C . . . M, are not followed by purchases, M . . . C (227–28). The logic of the hoard is therefore immanent to the logic of circulation. Moreover, the potential for hoards of money, as indeed the potential of money per se as an independent form of value, gives rise to a desire for money for its own sake as a representation of wealth (229–30). Marx is far from clear about why individuals would seek to make this desire a reality. He seems more interested in what happens, what is expressed socially, when money hoards form. In short, this is that "the social power becomes the private power of private persons" (230). The social power referred to is, of course, the social labor embodied in commodities, something money taps into in its being "the equivalent form of value," that into which can be converted any commodity. But bundled into this idea is the notion that social labor is not merely what commodities embody. Social labor is the productive capacity of the society as such and the ongoing development of this capacity. The power expressed in hoarded money—and in the very capacity to hoard, since hoarding is immanent to circulation—is therefore the development of the society itself. Marx also notes that social power accrues to money because money can buy anything without leaving a trace of what in particular was sold for it (229). This makes possible more and more kinds of things—more and more earthly matter—entering money's orbit, becoming representable by it. These then are the possibilities that become the property of private persons. The hoard is not simply private wealth stored up but social-historical time and space possessed by the private person. Thus, a breach is signaled in what value is ostensibly about, at least in one manner of reckoning (about to fly apart). Value works, we think, to distribute things in some sensible way, being an expression of equality among equal commodity producers, because it makes it possible for different sorts of commodity goods to be fairly exchanged. Immanent to this situation is money emerging as the one commodity equal to all others and therefore standing for a sort of equality. And yet precisely because it is a thingly equality, money can be laid hold of. This means that the form taken by equality can itself be taken hold of and yanked out of the fraternity of equality: the representative of value betrays value. This is predicated on the very manner in which equality is established— socially necessarily labor time, abstract labor. In Marx's analysis it is precisely putting this in motion in the form of money and the market that dissolves this equality, which is to say that equality in the commodity society is self-dissolving, a sandman that disintegrates under pressure of trying to stand. There is no exploitation of one person by another in this scenario of private gain. And so, quite extraordinarily, nonequality becomes the appearance that equality takes. What Marx is doing in launching this distinctive concept of value before that of capital value is in a sense accepting the way the commodity society sees itself (as a society of equals) in order to see if this vision is sustainable on its own terms. Can the putative society of equals be a society of equals and a commodity society at the same time? Impossible, he says. Even when we imagine that a commodity society, predicated on abstract labor, is not a capitalist society, predicated more fundamentally on forms of wage labor, things do not hold up as we imagine they do. We might as well imagine, he writes, that "all Catholics can be popes" (161n26).

The analysis does not end there. As we continue looking through the window of simple circulation at the money form of social power, when it is hoarded or held in reserve, we see its enormous costs. The money hoard and the act of hoarding run up against a fundamental antagonism inhering in money as the equivalent form. Money, as we know, potentially represents every, and any, kind of commodity. But the amount of money available in society in order for this potential to become real is limited. This *general* antagonism comes to rest in the *person* of the hoarder. Consider that under the rules of simple circulation, the hoarder can retrieve only so much money from the market as the commodity he throws into it is worth. On these terms the only way for the hoarder to accumulate money is to sacrifice the wants of the flesh and live on less. "Work, thrift, and greed are therefore his three cardinal virtues, and to sell much and buy little is the sum of his political economy" (231). Marx calls this the "Sisyphean task: accumulation" (231). If simple circulation looks like C . . . M . . . C, then the hoarder moves through the circuit like C . . . M . . . c (m)—that is, sell one's commodity, don't spend too much of the proceeds, thereby saving money, and on and on as the hoard grows: C . . . M . . . c (m) . . . C . . . M . . . c (m') . . . C . . . M . . . c (M) . . . C . . . M . . . c(M') . . . . The hoarder is a reflex of the antagonism of the equivalent form, with the difference from capital circulation being that M becomes M' on the back of the hoarder. The hoarder solves the fundamental antagonism I have described by reversing its terms—that is, by showing there can be more money than there are commodities and proving that money is the best form of value of all. The antagonism comes crashing down on the body of the hoarder, however, who can watch her hoard grow only by diminishing herself. Value then reaches its limit—is shown its limit—in the very body of the personage who wants it most. And both suffer for it.

We can see the problem even better if we think not so much of the hoarder individually but of the commodity society as a whole hoarding. Consider that money does its job best as a representative of value when it's in circulation, demonstrating that it is indeed the universal equivalent. But in order for this powerful thing to be displayed itself, in order to show that it is not simply caught up in circulation but has a semiautonomy within circulation, it must come to a stop somewhere, must show itself as a kind of fixity. Although the individual hoarder relishes this display of the potential power she has amassed (despite its cost to herself, although this cost also puts, sickly, her ingenuity on display), when raised to a social level this display takes on a different form, money reserves and credit. Marx argues that the commodity society, instead of fixing the problem of the hoard (something it could not do anyway, since the hoard is immanent in the value form), needs the hoard for a specific and practical reason. Because every purchase is not followed by a sale and vice versa, there must be hoards to serve as reserves of money to keep the commodities stream flowing and social reproduction proceeding apace (231–32). But if the option to not spend on either production or consumption is exercised often enough or in just the "right" ways, clearly some reserve of money must form beforehand, to be dipped into to keep things going. In keeping such reserves, the commodity society demonstrates its money power to itself, money (value) takes on a for-its-own-sake quality—a semiautonomy. Under these conditions, Marx argues, money as an independent power in and over society is intensified even further. Will the hoard be too small? Too big? Where will it be? Who will control it, and whom will it control? And if we look outside the domestic sphere—that is, beyond the boundaries of individual states to the international sphere, where gold and silver are the only world money—we also see the need for a hoard, a reserve, that greases the wheels of global commerce (240–44). But for all of this, a hoard is still a hoard. And with this is the irony that in order for money to function, it must . . . not function. Gold (and silver) are set aside from all other commodities, so they serve as universal equivalents by being continually pumped through the collective body of commodity society. But now, the equivalent form must be set *alongside* its own circulation. Value as a concept expressing the flows of equivalent matter, of matter rendered equivalent and commensurate, becomes increasingly inelegant and ungainly and, as Eric Sheppard and Trevor Barnes show, not very value-like at all.[16]

It is now, given Marx's discussion of the hoard, an easy and obvious step to credit as a necessary feature of commodity circulation (234–38). Credit becomes the "means of payment" to reconnect sales and purchases, to hold fast the C . . . M . . . C circuit. As Marx writes, "While hoarding, considered as an independent form of self-enrichment, vanishes with the advance of bourgeois society, it grows at the same time in the form of the accumulation of a reserve fund of the means of payment [credit]" (240). But we must not imagine that credit solves the problems expressed by the hoard, that Marx, after the long march of part 1 of *Capital*, has in mind giving the gift of equilibrium to the commodity society that has hungered for it so! Credit *disturbs* equivalence—the equivalence that was always-already never there. Because sales and purchases of commodities involve commodities produced over varying production times, at various places, and in various industries, credit money falls out of sequence with the values it ostensibly represents.

> Money which represents commodities long withdrawn from circulation, continues to circulate. Commodities circulate, but their equivalent in money does not appear until some future date. Moreover, the debts contracted each day, and the payments falling due on the same day, are entirely incommensurable magnitudes. (237)

To what end? Credit, meant to resolve the contradiction that is latent in simple circulation, instead devolves into irrelevance when crisis, also latent in this form, emerges. On the eve of crisis,

> the bourgeois, drunk with prosperity and arrogantly certain of himself, has just declared that money is purely an imaginary creation. "Commodities alone are money," he said. But now the opposite cry resounds over the markets of the world: only money is a commodity. As the hart pants after fresh water, so pants his soul after money, the only wealth. In a crisis, the antithesis between commodities and their value-form, money, is raised to the level of an absolute contradiction. Hence money's form of appearance is here also a matter of indifference. The monetary famine remains whether payments have to be made in gold or in credit-money, such as bank-notes. (236–37)

By the end of part 1, in which Marx investigates the use of gold and silver as universal (world) money, the hoard makes a reappearance. The progress of bourgeois society in fact demands that supposed vanished forms be dragged along for the ride. If hoarding might have been written off as the self-defeating lust of a few private individuals, it reemerges as a social necessity. Thus, "just as every country needs a reserve of money for its internal circulation, so too it requires one for circulation in the world market. The functions of hoards, therefore, arise in part out of the function of money as medium of payment and circulation internally, and in part out of its function as a world currency" (243). "Whenever these hoards are strikingly above their average level, this is, with some exceptions, an indication of stagnation in the circulation of commodities, i.e., of an interruption in the flow of their metamorphoses" (244). Part 1 ends there. Credit (means of payment) and hoards are each mired in uncertainty and guesswork. Value produces forms that are not very value-like at all. The only way for value to appear for its own sake is if somebody, everybody, suffers for it.

In the act and body of the hoard, Marx has still another lesson to tell that is as true of simple circulation, C . . . M . . . C, as it is of the capital form of circulation, M . . . C . . . M'. Money is the only form that the equivalent form of value can take. Thus, in the example of hoarding, despite the value of gold (money) going up and down, gold (money) is still the primary value form worth hoarding. Gold remains gold (money remains money) regardless of its value and remains the hoarder's object of choice. One may wish to hoard a different form of equivalent value, but one cannot. It *is* the equivalent form. Though its value may rise and fall with respect to the other commodity values it can command, more gold (money) is still worth more than less gold (money) (230). Again, there's nowhere else to go along the value chain, nothing better to choose among the gamut of commodities that present themselves. It remains the universal equivalent and represents not simply a subset of commodities but them all. In choosing to hoard gold, one has already hoarded everything else. Gold (money) is then its own measure, excepting the nasty supply problem or economic crisis I have noted. (Or as Marx writes later in the chapter on the formula for capital, M . . . M′, money is in a private relationship with itself (256)—which is preferable, since value has itself no value. The equivalent form of value has no other value through which to represent itself.) What this means is that even though gold holds a certain power over the hoarder, it can display this power only in a way that reveals its own limit, this simply being that the equivalent form of value has to take a form at all. We have only to conjure a small counterfactual to glimpse the absurdity at the bottom of this. Suppose a society where production proceeds according to some settled plan by which the social division of labor is thought through by the associated laborers (as Marx calls them) in accordance with their perceived needs as a society. And suppose, as Marx would insist, that this is not a commodity society, with all that that implies. Therefore, it's not a money society and not a society that predicates production, distribution, and earnings on the strangled basis of equivalences of average labor times and, thus, is forced to haphazardly regard the particular use values actually in distribution. But do suppose that the society nonetheless produces (necessarily so). Would one hoard linen? Coats? Shoes? Brandy? Iron? Why? The existence of a hoard would, on Marx's terms, scarcely be thinkable under conditions of associated labor: neither linen nor coats nor shoes immanently contain the hoard, since none of these represents social power broadly. The mere hint of a hoard would signify some sort of imbalance and prompt a collective concern with the social division of labor. It is different in the commodity society. The money hoard is, as Marx theorizes it, the ruse of a social power that presents itself as purposed for private possession. But once actually held privately, it ceases to be social power. So there you have it. Or not. "It is different in the commodity society," which is not a statement that value is irrelevant to the noncommodity society of associated producers.

Values in Motion

I have been attempting an initial appreciation of the life of value in *Capital*, before Marx rolls out the red carpet for the grand entrance of surplus value, capital, and wage labor. There is something paradoxical in this because I agree that a starkly different reading is possible. This other, more accepted reading is that the first iteration of the value concept in capital *presupposes* the more complex forms elaborated later (that is to say, capital and all its moments): variable and constant capital, fixed and circulating capital, surplus value, rent, credit, interest, profit of enterprise, etc. Such a reading holds that the true meaning of value exists and is revealed only retroactively after comprehending the totality of Marx's capital corpus. In Patrick Murray's words, for example, "As *Capital* unfolds, we discover that the generalization of the production of wealth in the commodity form presupposes the more complex value categories of capital and wage-labor."[17] We read this statement as saying not only that a fully developed commodity society would be a society based only on the "complex categories of capital and wage-labor" but also that understanding Marx's very idea of value, to be comprehended properly, presupposes its fully elaborated, single idea.[18] But what I am trying to get at here is that a lot happens of extraordinary interest before those suppositions come into full force, even if we do not discount them. Not the least is that the polyvalent hearing given to value in the first part of *Capital* raises questions by which capital and capitalism themselves can partly be judged.

In that sense, what's been achieved so far? An initial point is that value is not simply the time of abstract labor but also the forms through which abstract labor appears or fails to appear. What we are seeing in Marx's value-in-use is that these forms are both inadequate to value (any present amount of money or present amount and kind of commodity cannot represent the quaky terrain of value) and exceed value at the same moment (the money form takes on characteristics, behaves in ways, that depart from its being merely a value form). Value, Marx adds, is not something we are aware of "doing." The essential, or an essential, feature of value is that we, its actors, are unaware of its existence, unaware of rendering labor as value by abstracting it. What the commodity fetish idea adds is that even if we were aware that labor is rendered abstract, we could not *not* do this. Even if—as we'll see in the next chapter—we knew about and planned for abstracting labor, we would still have just that, a plan that could not fulfill its own promises and that would limit alternative courses of action. Even on their own account, therefore, the producing members of the commodity society find their system, as well as their relationships and individual places within it, disturbed. And they would find them disturbed regardless of whether they competed with each on the market or produced for each other directly but privately. Money, the form taken by the value they have produced, has its own independent power and cannot represent them.

In other words, the commodity fetish has a trickster-like quality. Even if one wanted to organize society along commodity lines, things still wouldn't work. The society of commodity-producing equals cannot in fact be brought into existence. The commodity fetish is not so much a lesson about the importance of fairness, equality of social members, or social knowledge about conditions as it is a lesson about independent powers—an independent power, money in this case, that is paradoxical in that it can neither be done away with nor actually brought into functional existence. It is, as Marx notes in another context, a "nightmare weighing on the brains of the living." (But if this is so, Marx's insight is actually very heavily freighted. It invites us to think of the unplanned commodity society in terms of its opposite, a planned society. What's to keep a social plan from becoming a sort of independent power? What's to prevent the eternal return of the fetish? And what's the proper response to it? We are also invited to consider why if the commodity society is doomed at its outset, it doesn't pretty soon implode.)

Recalling, however, the *comparative* context in which Marx places the commodity society in the second cut at the commodity fetish, the concept of value seems to be released from belonging to any one kind of society. Perhaps the point is just that Marx, without saying precisely so, has built multiple homes or frames for value, one describing what happens in commodity society (value assumes many forms), another describing what cannot happen there (commodity society cannot sustain value), still another that evaluates commodity society on the basis of (a still deferred) value, which could make its appearance in some other sort of society, and one in which value is not something meant to appear at all (chapter 2 explores these last two possibilities). Faced with such an archive of possibilities, the temptation is to choose the theoretical tradition felt to hold the greatest explanatory promise.[19] Another choice would be to argue that value is just a conceptual disaster for political economy.[20] Or perhaps value's failure is broader still. Marcus Doel, taking aim as much at Antonio Negri's autonomism as David Harvey's historical-geographical materialism, writes, "The challenge that faces political economists and historical-geographical materialists is to let value, and especially surplus value, go: without resentment and without nostalgia. It is not that value (in all its manifestations) is fated to return to its rightful owner and proper place (living labor). Rather, value is destined to dissipate."[21] In essence, Doel is concerned that Marx's notion of value begins with such a reduced notion of the (capitalist) world's implicit profusion that the idea of profusion, when it finally emerges (in the guise of surplus value), is not recognized as reflecting the conceptual reduction with which it began. Fair enough. How to *think* capitalism is in fact enormously difficult. The fate of all concepts is that they never exhaust the things and the processes they attempt to name, while completely missing or occluding other things and processes. As far as value goes, Marx would try to have it both ways. He shows precisely how the commodity society reduces the world by invoking a problematic of value that he would insist is not nearly so constrained. For now, I prefer a temporary, metaphorical resolution to these conundrums that thinks of these value alternatives in prismatic terms—the opacity of any one notion of value can be lessened by scrutinizing it from the perspective of another. I don't propose a full round of such scrutiny in a short book, only enough to suggest, I hope, that the common sense of Marx takes on a more interesting coloration if it is many sided. Or if you like, let's just see if it makes sense to accept that different tropes and deployments of value strike different political points.

2

The Politics of Capitalist "Totality" in a More-Than-Capitalist World

Footnotes That Travel

The argument that value, properly understood, presupposes capital and all the forms Marx elaborates for it in the chapters and volumes of *Capital* beyond those I have considered so far is sometimes deployed to emphasize that when Marx analyzes simple circulation (C . . . M . . . C), he does not mean that such a social form actually exists or is a historical precursor to capitalism proper. Rather than outlining a separate mode of simple commodity production or independent/petty commodity production, Marx is developing a first cut at the value theory that contains the presumption of further theoretical development. Such a reading of value *as* internalized anticipation should not be considered wrong. It is, however, right in a way that obfuscates Marx leveraging simple circulation numerous times for purposes of describing and critiquing some of the utopian socialist thought of his day.[1] These are socialist experiments whose goal is, Marx argues, to have money directly express value by indexing it to labor time and, thus, labor money. This opens up Marx's concept of value to an alternative reading in which it is addressed to and emerges from within the multiples of political economy in Marx's time. To put this differently, Marx seems to be implicitly rendering modern bourgeois society as itself a diverse manifestation to be captured in the value concept. The gambit then is that Marx's value-in-use is not collapsible into the value-in-motion of capital. This is a confusing point, however, for Marx himself writes that the model of value that emerges from the analysis of commodity exchange inevitably points to the model he develops of capitalist production. I will try, therefore, to approach the matter as carefully as possible.

Not long into *Capital*, readers might notice Marx's having made a number of short asides addressed to various socialist utopian schemes developed by John Gray, John Bray, Robert Owen, and others, but most especially Pierre-Joseph Proudhon.[2] These asides typically are footnotes that eviscerate these schemes because of their poor understanding of the relationship between commodities and money—in particular, schemes that would try to allocate commodities justly on the basis of labor money or the time chit, as it's sometimes called. "This philistine utopia," Marx writes in chapter 1, "is depicted in the socialism of Proudhon, which, as I have shown elsewhere, does not even possess the merit of originality, but was in fact developed far more successfully long before Proudhon by Gray, Bray, and others. Even so, wisdom of this kind is still rife in certain circles under the name of 'science'" (161n26). It is impossible, he writes in chapter 2, that "Proudhonian socialism" could perpetuate commodity production yet abolish the antagonism between money and commodities, "since money exists only in and through this antagonism. . . . One might just as well abolish the Pope while leaving Catholicism in existence" (181n4). His writing goes similarly in the other places where these notes and asides appear, leading the philosopher and historian Jacques Rancière to point out about *Capital* that "in a sense . . . what Marx wants to demonstrate in the book is achieved in the very first chapter." In a certain political context, namely the struggles among competing socialisms, the important point about value theory is not its identification with capital but its formulation as an escape route from capital. "The crucial thing here," Rancière writes, "is not the exposé of surplus value; everyone knows that secret, and scrupulous distinctions between the value of labor and the value of labor power have no importance *in this context*. The crucial thing is destroying in advance Proudhon's solution to surplus value, which is the free and equal exchange of labor between producers. . . . Once [Marx] has established that the equivalent form of the commodity is an exclusive form, the game is over. Proudhonism is impossible."[3]

Behind the scenes of *Capital* is that Marx had forged a critique of utopian socialism in the 1840s—*The Poverty of Philosophy*—and a decade later made this a central preoccupation of "The Chapter on Money" in the *Grundrisse*, the notebooks Marx made in preparation for *Capital*. It appears, then, that much of what is contained in that chapter had been reduced to footnotes and asides during the trip to the more finished work of *Capital*. As Martin Nicolaus explains, *Capital* finds Marx's analysis of the socialists reduced to footnotes because Marx reconsidered the starting point of his critique of political economy and had done so even while compiling the *Grundrisse*. The critique of the socialists was ultimately regarded as a false start once Marx had figured out the intimate relationship between the commodity, abstract labor, and money. So rather than begin with money, he would need, in *Capital*, to begin with the concrete category of the commodity. If anything, though, "The Chapter on Money" shows that the tension was not perfectly resolved.[4] The chapter begs us to travel back, to rescale those footnotes back to their previous size. Doing so brings into relief that instead of the analysis of value being steeped in the critique of capital and pointing directly and resolutely toward capital, as if it had no other destiny, it is already steeped in the analysis of socialist ideas that would go beyond capital. Furthermore, when Marx finds fault with these schemes, it is not that he simply reduces them to capital (even though, as we'll see, at a certain point he claims otherwise). They are different from capitalist value, even being worse than it. In working toward a better-resolved value problem, Marx introduces the idea that in order to make value real, to solve the problem that value presents to the commodity society and to bad socialism and make it truly appear, a solution must be found that abolishes the warped premises of the commodity and of the utopians and finds a new premise for the society of associated labor. This is all done in value terms—that is, in its language and its idioms. But it's also all something of a high-wire act. We will find, I think, not a single, unfolding argument but Marx struggling to walk the tightrope between the idea of economic totality (or the internally related totalities of production and circulation) at one pole and the practice of a theory building whose steps lack political closure at the other pole. It is as if one pole is placed smack in the middle of the "immense collection of commodities" and the other pole in the middle of the collection of political-economic alternatives of the time. Value theory could begin at either point, but eventually the traverse beckons. This tension is less theoretically worked out than practically demonstrated by Marx. In any event, we can say with some certainty at the end that capital in no way simply confines what Marx is doing with value. This does not mean he is oblivious to or forgetful of his concept of value in capital. Rather, value is an engagement with the multiple economic schemes that characterize modernity and seem to lure Marx away from a too-totalizing vision. It is this unhinging of value from capital that is one of the ways capital and value do not form a unity.

The Financial Crisis (of Utopian Socialism)

What, then, does Marx do in the *Grundrisse*'s chapter on money? What are the arguments, and what is their sequence? The chapter begins with the question of how to develop an accurate analysis of and radical response to a financial crisis. Marx opens with immediate reference to one of Proudhon's followers, Alfred Darimon, and his 1856 treatise *De la réforme des banques*. Darimon's idea for bank reform is to see if the supply of money can be matched to the needs of circulation. Marx considers this impossible, as banks must live up to the broader requirements of the commodity society. In particular, in order to grease the wheels of commerce, an excess of money (a hoard) is necessary. Had Darimon used his data properly, Marx argues, the point would have been obvious. "But then," he writes, hinting at some willful ignorance on Darimon's part, if not an ulterior motive, "the question would have been deflated from the socialist heights down to the practical bourgeois plains. . . . What a come down!" (120). Using some of the same data sources as Darimon, Marx gives multiple examples of how the ordinary course of commodity exchange, nationally and internationally, must result in imbalances of coin, paper money, and commodity supply and demand (120–22, 125–30). This gives rise to what he regards as the fundamental question.

> Can the existing relations of production and the relations of distribution which correspond to them be revolutionized by a change in the instrument of circulation, in the organization of circulation? Further question: Can such a transformation of circulation be undertaken without touching the existing relations of production and the social relations which rest on them? (122)

If the answer to the second question is no—and he considers it is—then we get the "collapse of the doctrine that proposes tricks of circulation as a way of, on the one hand, avoiding the violent character of these social changes, and, on the other, of making these changes appear to be not a presupposition but a gradual result of the transformations in circulation" (122). There is no understanding, in other words, of the "inner connections between relations of production, of distribution, and of circulation" (122). Even if there is the desire to change all of these relations, they could not get away with the claim that changes to circulation could become the basis for social change at large.

Then follows an interesting embellishment of the fundamental question, which must now ask

> whether the different civilized forms of money—metallic, paper, credit money, labor money [the last identifies the socialist form]—can accomplish what is demanded of them *without suspending the very relation of production which is expressed in the category money*, and whether it is a self-contradictory demand to wish to get around essential determinants of a relation by means of formal modifications? (123; emphasis added)

Obviously, Marx's view is that indeed money, to be what it is, would have to suspend the relations of production of the commodity society (the accidental nature of abstract labor) to which it is internally related. (Though phrased as a question, there is no better and no more succinct statement than this one that commodity society is unable to produce value.) As to the hope that "formal modifications" could bring about fundamental change, it would then be impossible, as Marx has already argued, that those relations of production could be gotten around by tinkering with the very institution whose purpose is to secure those relations.

Now, Marx's critique so far—just a few scarce pages into the chapter—is vested in the idea of value as a set of internal relations having to do with capitalism. As we read on, the curious thing is that he does not really find fault with the circulation solution proposed by the utopians, on the basis that they leave capitalist production relations untouched, if by these relations we mean *class*. The questions Marx raises are instead sidestepped. It is important to see how and to what end, for indeed the point here is not so much capitalism as Proudhonism and what can be learned through its specific demolition.

Consider Marx's beef with the utopian socialists and Proudhon, in particular. Against Proudhon and his notion of a bedrock value for metallic currency, Marx writes that gold and silver do not have "authentic value in contrast to the other commodities" (i.e., the rise and fall in prices of other commodities affect the amount of gold or silver needed to buy them). Metallic money and paper also appreciate and depreciate (129–30). Having removed a sort of floor notion of value, Marx rapidly goes through a regressing series of questions and answers. How can depreciation of money, a concern of Proudhon, be avoided? Avoid giving commodities prices. And how to avoid prices? Avoid attributing exchange value to commodities. But how can exchange value be avoided? Avoid bourgeois (commodity) production. And when Marx repeats something much like these steps in the *Grundrisse*'s analysis of the commodity fetish, he writes that Proudhon should have been able to figure all of this out (134). And more.

The value of gold, like all commodities, is determined by average labor time, but not the labor time reflected in the moment when it was made, as if a given piece of gold could carry with it into the future its present value. Rather, its value is determined by the "amount of labor time necessary at a given moment." And this is an ongoing moment. Moreover, if we add the general economic law that the productivity of labor tends to increase, we get the constant depreciation of gold. These tendencies seriously damage the plans of Proudhon and company, who propose that paper money be directly tied to labor time. At first such a proposal appears advantageous. Given the tendency for labor to become more productive,

> the chit of paper which represents [an hour of labor] would rise in buying power. . . . Paper labor money would enjoy a constant appreciation. And that is precisely what we are after; the worker would reap the joys of rising productivity of his labor, instead of creating proportionately more alien wealth and devaluing himself as at present. Thus the socialists. But unfortunately, there arise some small scruples. (136)

Among these scruples is the probability that if money exists, even in the form of time chits, then these chits can be accumulated by individuals. The problem would be compounded by these individuals, not the entirety of workers, reaping an outsized share of productivity increases. We see the beginnings of a hoard in this form of socialism, then, together with the possibility that the hoard grows in power even when no more chits are added to it.

Alas, things get worse. The time chit proposes not only to remunerate labor at its value but also to match value and price. Marx considers this impossible and warns that much mischief would come of it. He reminds us that value is not labor time as such but socially average labor time, and a moving average of labor time over decades at that. For this reason market value is "always different, is always above or below this average value of a commodity. Market value equates itself with real value by means of constant non-equation of itself." Moreover, real value negates and contradicts itself insofar as it meddles with the value of already produced commodities, constantly rerendering them in appreciating or depreciating terms, as the case may be (137). Marx concludes that the "value of the commodity itself exists only in this up-and-down movement of commodity prices" (138). What are the implications for the time chit? "The time-chit, representing *average labor time*, would never correspond to or be convertible to *actual labor time*; i.e., the amount of labor time objectified in a commodity would never command a quantity of labor time equal to itself" (139). This would make explicit a confusion that money, in its regular bourgeois form, happily masks. The time chit would abolish what Marx sees as the necessary contradiction between money price and value: that price cannot immediately reflect value. Money prices allow a necessary veiling of exchange relations, whereas time chits would produce a confusion that "would reach new heights altogether" (139).

Value in this rendering, wherein labor is dynamic, stretches across time and space and has no existence apart from this span, certainly not in any particular moment of time or at any point in space. Value therefore cannot appear (i.e., take form) as what it is and yet is required to take form if it's to hint at its existence and mean anything at all. Money in the commodity society allows these contradictions to slide. The time chit does not, however, and is actually a *worse* system: in its way it serves a money function while actually being worse than money. Value, were it to be the *actual*, thinglike representation of labor, does not so much give rise to capitalism as it gives rise to something even more confusing. But consider the odd status of the concept of value. The form seemingly best suited to manifest value and show what it is—namely, labor money—could not do so, just as bourgeois money cannot do so. This places us in the ironic situation in which Marx's labor theory of value, which is supposedly the same as capitalism, is worse than capitalism. We have another manifestation of the disunity of value and capital or, at the minimum, a very odd situation in which value exceeds the bounds of the theory of capital.

We will see how Marx deals with this momentarily. But there is further exploratory work to do. Why, for example, does the exchange value of commodities, or just two commodities, require a third commodity, money, as a mediating device (140–45)? Commodities are in some sense initially doomed by their physical form or, specifically, by the problem physical form poses when the point of commodities—all commodities—is that they are exchangeable for each other on the basis of necessary labor time. Forgetting for the moment that Marx has already made mincemeat of this equivalence, money is a brilliant mediator for such a contradiction. Insofar as money represents almost any quantity of labor time, it can buy things that any other physical commodity cannot buy. For example, consider the exchange between a barrel of oil and a bible without money in existence. If I had a barrel of oil (and who has just one barrel?) and wanted to buy a bible (one is probably enough), I could not in fact buy only one bible but would have to buy the barrel's equivalent, perhaps ten bibles. This is because I could not divide up the barrel into labor time equivalents of one bible. It is different with money, which can be minted (or printed) in small and large denominations alike. I could sell my barrel for money and then buy my bible or, perhaps, something else. Pieces of money representing "fractional parts of labor time," as Marx puts it, can do things that no other commodity can do and therefore can represent commodity exchange universally (144). More abstractly, the "contradiction between the commodity's particular natural qualities [steam engine, bible, and every other commodity thing] and its general social qualities [any commodity must be exchangeable for any other] contains from the beginning the possibility that these two separated forms in which the commodity exists are not convertible into one another" (147)—unless, of course, there is money as a *numeraire*. But note that "as soon as money has become an external thing alongside the commodity, the exchangeability of the commodity for money becomes bound up with external conditions which may or may not be present" (147). Marx follows with a discussion of some familiar constraints—that sales are not necessarily followed by purchases and vice versa, that the desire for exchange for the sake of exchange might trump the desire to exchange for the sake of consuming, that the money supply may or may not be sufficiently present, and that any or all of these may manifest themselves.

In a few short pages (140–51), fewer than in *Capital*, he shows how the widening circle of exchange relations leads to the necessity of the money form of value, which leads to the increasing potential of money to become an independent power in society and, thus, to the potential for the money form to introduce its own problems and contradictions and cease to merely represent labor time, its origin. Before this discussion, Marx argues that value cannot in fact *be* in capitalism; now we have watched as the required universal form of value descends into the impractical bourgeois plains.

Marx returns to the time chit and what ails it and, indeed, to money and how to fix the value problem that inheres in it. He moves in two directions, one showing how the time chit, done right, must lead to either associated production or despotism, the other taking the concept of money and turning it into the concept of production in common (communism). A bank issuing time chits could work properly, Marx argues, only if it had no competition from competing currencies, from competing labor regimes whose productivity varied, or from substitute commodities unrepresented by time chits but circulating along with the commodities that were backed by time chits. In other words, the possibility of competing value forms would have to be eliminated, as they would potentially undermine the value of the time chit.

> Precisely seen, then, the bank would be not only the
> general buyer and seller, but also the general producer.
> In fact either it would be a despotic ruler of production
> and trustee of distribution, or it would indeed be nothing
> more than a board which keeps the books and accounts
> for a society producing in common. (155)

Marx takes on the time chit concept to undermine and open it up at the same time. And he does this in an indeterminate way, underscoring the openness of the social field itself and the dangers of clinging to, indeed fetishizing, independent forms of social power. (But he suggests more than this, I think. He does not deny the necessity of social forms, of institutions and numbers [e.g., "a board which keeps the books and accounts"]. There seemingly is in Marx a need for mirrors of society's own design, reflections and representations that show to society what measures it consists of.[5] Value and Marx stalk and shadow each other each step of the way.)

Marx wraps up his comments on the time chit bank by emphasizing that movements against capitalism and for a society of associated production would need to choose the right element of capital to eliminate and the proper historical potentials to seize for purposes of transformation. He is not terribly specific as to what this means exactly but is emphatic that capitalism is in the business of producing these potentials. In passages that reappear in only slightly changed form in the first volume of *Capital*, he writes in the *Grundrisse* of how bourgeois society and commodity production, as destructive as they are, also involve the making of the new individual and social capacities (162). Though not yet being lived, these could nonetheless emerge from the mere fact of the social bonds and the increase of productive forces made through and necessitated by commodity production and exchange (161). The advantage of capitalist commodity production over utopian socialism is that the nonnecessity of money to directly express value in the commodity society allows this society to blunder blindly along, if progressively, whereas utopian socialism would in a sense try to let value and its money form know each other too much.

And what about the second direction in which Marx takes his analysis of money? Following the time chit discussion, he again reminds his readers that money, as a measure of price, must be distinct from labor time (163–69). The meaning of labor time (value) is in its averages, whereas price is something paid now. One can no more freeze the moment of now than still the moving average. But he then turns the tables and seriously poses the question he writes off fifty pages earlier. What if labor time really could be money?

If labor time, which is predicated on abstract labor, called general labor here, were to be regarded as identical to money, then labor immediately and directly would need to be recognized as general in the sphere of production itself, not indirectly recognized as general through exchange (171–73). So if the goal or sine qua non of commodity production is that it fixes upon the ability of labor to be rendered abstract, then in effect what Marx says is, fine, let's really make it so. Before exchange happens, let's admit that society most fundamentally produces itself through its active transformation of the surrounding world and that this is immediately always-already a social process, too: we cannot subsist except by engaging the nonhuman environment and doing so in a social context that is prior to the individual. This is our general condition: we generally exist already in production. That is to say, we have a common (though not identical) existence there. But this commonality remains abstract so long as we do not actively engage with each other on what is to be produced, what results are desired, how individuals are to realize themselves socially, and so on. We must actively and intentionally mediate our existence in production rather than accidentally and retroactively in exchange. There, in the sphere of production, let's agree upon what the society needs, what a meaningful life is, and what it requires, and then, let's have distributional arrangements predicated on those ideas, rather than arising accidentally. (The idea of exchange as a separate sphere then goes by the wayside.)

Marx is saying that money, while assigned the role of recognizing abstract labor, does so in the wrong place, the wrong sphere. When we turn this upside-down world right side up, we see abstract labor very differently and the social bonds that intensify and widen in the commodity society in an entirely new light, too. And although the utopian socialists *could* see this, they don't. Marx puts the matter thus: time chit money makes a "demand [that] can be satisfied under conditions where it can no longer be raised" (172). But what about labor time as such? After all, Marx is interested in the question of how labor time really could become money. We've seen him give an answer that radically alters the meaning of money—its meaning *is* its nonnecessity. Still, in communal production, Marx writes, "determination of labor time remains essential." "Economy of time," he writes, becomes "law, to an even higher degree," but in a manner that "is essentially different from a measurement of exchange values (labor or products) by labor time" (173). The core problem concerns what it is that labor time counts. This is interesting. Marx takes us back to the distinction between the difference and the relation between labor's quantitative and qualitative aspects (the difference between abstract and concrete labor). In commodity exchange the former is brought to the foreground and becomes what counts. So long as only time is valued, there is no (immediate) need to be worried about the actual use values produced and exchanged—for example, whether they are really needed, whether certain concrete labor skills are overemphasized at the expense of others, whether there are too many of one kind and not enough of another (the old problem of imbalance). But if labor time counts qualitatively—if we immerse ourselves in the problem of how labor time is concretely spent—then we confront these issues directly rather than incidentally and haphazardly. We would then have not just a "higher degree" of the old "law" but a very different law indeed: purposeful and common control of the "economy of time."

Where does value stand now? Marx gives us a rendering of the concept that is different from what we get in *Capital* or, at least, the dominant way of reading *Capital*. Traditionally, this book is read along a certain grain that says value leads to capital. (The *Grundrisse* can also be read in this way, too.) In this reading, capital subsumes and transforms anything else that might be meant by "value." In the previous chapter, I suggest reading *Capital* differently from that grain, however, by arguing we can read capitalism (the commodity society) as the departure further and further away from value (in the normative problem-solved sense); capital instead develops the nonbeing of value in ever more tangled, absurd, albeit ingenious ways. It can but wreak havoc upon the very relations that are trying (insofar as there is a sort of unfolding logic in capital) to gain expression in social form. This situation opens up a reading of value as that which might have some other sort of existence than its nonbeing in capital, its nonbeing in the very middle of that "immense collection of commodities." With "The Chapter on Money" in the *Grundrisse*, it is otherwise yet again. Here is a Marx who thinks value in the matrix of contemporary debates about economic practices and plans. And what has emerged is a different fate for the value idea. Its practical home is much less the commodity society and much less what Marx has dubbed utopian socialism and much more the society of associated production.

". . . Points beyond Itself"

As Marx works to complete his analysis of exchange, money, and prices (i.e., the circulation of commodities considered as a totality) in the chapter on money he argues that the precondition of this sphere is the sphere of production, of relations of production. Thus, the chapter on money "points beyond itself towards the economic relations that are posited as relations of production" (227). Therefore, in the subsequent chapter on capital, his point is that because exchange must ultimately involve the circulation of use values, destined for consumption, circulation as a totality has no way of renewing (positing) itself on its own and must inevitably confront the totality of production. This is the second time Marx raises the question of production in the *Grundrisse*, now confronting it as a totality of a particular kind. It is yet another opportunity (so soon!) to see that the work of value is not everything the mainline interpretation thinks. The key word here is *totality*. Marx is concerned with the totality of circulation and the totality of production, en route to discovering that the latter is the dominant site in the totality of capitalism. What he finds out though, without saying as much, is that capitalist society is not itself a totality (the utopian socialists are evidence of this) and that this is another warrant for the multiplicity of value. This means that the return of totality does not quiet all that Marx seems to want to say on the subject of value. The point can be dramatized by reflecting on the passage in the "Chapter on Capital" where Marx brings the totality of circulation to its limit point and concludes that circulation certainly must point elsewhere:

Since money is only the realization of exchange value, and since the system of exchange values has realized itself only in a developed money system, or inversely, the money system can indeed only be the realization of this system of freedom and equality. As measure, money only gives the equivalent its specific expression, makes it into an equivalent in form, as well. A distinction of form does, it is true, arise within circulation: the two exchangers appear in the different roles of buyer and seller; exchange value appears once in its general form, in the form of money, then again in its particular form, in the natural commodity, now with a price; but, first of all these forms alternate; circulation itself creates not disequation, but only an equation, a suspension of the merely negated difference. The inequality is only a purely formal one. Finally, even equality now posits itself tangibly, in money as medium of circulation, where it appears now in one hand, now in another, and is indifferent to this appearance. Each appears towards the other as an owner of money, and as regards the process of exchange, as money itself. Thus indifference and equal worthiness are expressly contained in the form of the thing. The particular natural difference which was contained in the commodity is extinguished, and constantly becomes extinguished by circulation. A worker who buys commodities for 3s. appears to the seller in the same function, in the same equality—in the form of 3s.— as the king who does the same. All distinction between them is extinguished. The seller *qua* seller appears only as owner of a commodity of the price of 3s., so that both are completely equal; only that the 3s. exist here in the form of silver, there again in the form sugar, etc. In the third form of money, a distinguishing quality might seem to enter between the subjects of the process. But in so far as money here appears as the material, as the general commodity of contracts, all distinction between the contracting parties, is rather, extinguished. In so far as money, the general form of wealth, becomes the object

of accumulation, the subject here appears to withdraw it
from circulation only to the extent that he does not withdraw commodities of an equal price from circulation.
Thus, if one individual accumulates and the other does
not, then none does it at the expense of the other. One
enjoys real wealth, the other takes possession of wealth
in its general form. If one grows impoverished and the
other grows wealthier, then this is of their own free will
and does not in any way arise from the economic relation, the economic connection as such, in which they are
placed in relation to one another. (246–47)

What is the implication of this passage? That anything odd,
anything contravening equality that happens during exchange,
is not part of the social function of exchange, per se—that is,
when we look at exchange only. For the sphere of exchange *is*
the sphere in which equality shows itself. Inequalities would be
due to subjective errors and misappraisals or individual superiority or cheating; they would be "irrelevant to the nature of the
relation as such." Irregularities apparently contravening equivalence "would *happen not because of the nature of the social
function in which they confront one another*" (241; emphasis
in original). But because circulation/exchange has its precondition in production—that is, it does not instantiate itself—Marx
can indeed say that circulation "points beyond itself" toward a
different totality and do so bluntly. "It is just as pious as it is stu-
pid to wish that exchange value would not develop into capital,
nor labor which produces exchange value into wage labor"—
yet another barb pointed at the utopian socialists (249).

But if all that is so—if the totality of the sphere of exchange
points only toward the totality of capitalist production relations, conceptually and in practice (and Marx here appears to
say this), and if the totality of production requires the totality
of circulation to mask the creation of surplus value and exploitation—then it is difficult to understand how Marx could have
already derived out of exchange relations, *considered by themselves,* a desire to move beyond the commodity society (and,
no less, get around the obstacle of a possible dictatorship) and

derived how such a society might be founded. In sum, Marx exposes the "piety and stupidity" of the utopian socialists, but his proof never depends on showing that their plans would become ever more capitalistic. He needs to show only that even time chit money could not represent value and that an independent form of social power would surely emerge.

This is symptomatic of the conflicted but highly strategic way Marx mobilizes the totality. Consider his comment on the concept of circulation as a directly political concept, a comment made in the *Grundrisse*'s chapter on money. In this chapter, during his analysis of the circulation of money and commodities, Marx shows how an alien power takes over society. And even though dealing with conscious individuals in this society, he notes that these individuals are engaged in social interactions that are "neither located in their conscious, nor subsumed under them as a whole." And because individuals are not free social individuals, they perceive their sociality to occur by chance or natural force. This leads Marx to conclude that "circulation as the first totality among the economic categories is well suited to bring this to light" (196–97). This comment is noteworthy because Marx has displayed an interest in showing that the discrete, individual steps taken toward a comprehensive, multiperspectival analysis (i.e., an analysis of how multiple totalities are sutured together through contradiction and displacement) can make their own political points. But these points are, it seems to me, more wandering and profligate than Marx admits. The case can be put thus: Marx wants to make the argument that the developed circulation of money must presume capitalist social relations of production (and be reproduced by them). The analysis of these production relations, the production totality, would then be necessary for showing that production by associated producers would be better. *But* the totalities and the articulation between them are more precocious than this—*a totality starts doing its political work before Marx completely frames it*. This is because the capitalist social formation as such is not a totality but a complex political formation, for which he apparently would like to account, that disrupts his own (seeming) mainline argument. What Marx does in the chapter on money is draw a line directly from the analysis of (utopian socialist) circulation to associated production. The attempt by utopian socialists to radicalize circulation, in Marx's hands, does indeed point beyond itself, but to production in common not to an analysis of the totality of capitalist production relations and then to the desire for production in common. For sure, such an analysis of capital does come. But it is now part of more socially complex considerations rather than the singular one of capital. (To put the point differently, in regarding money as a false start with which to begin *Capital*, because money properly emerges only from the concrete category of the commodity, Marx discounts the concrete event of contemporary socialist politics. It is not a denial but a trade-off, and yet a trade-off that marks value's plurality in *Capital* just the same.) As in the second cut at the commodity fetish in chapter 1, the diverse pathways of value talk in Marx must be appreciated rather than suppressed. One cannot avoid seeing Marx as almost an opportunist when it comes to his own thought. Never does he wait for the conclusions to his scientific theory to derive its political conclusions, while the latter, forever at the ready, interrupt and splinter the trajectory of value theory. And at times Marx seems to sacrifice these derivations for the sake of moving on to the next totality. And this is, finally, the source of a peculiar irony. In the *Grundrisse* the totality of production requires, it seems, a cleaned-up, reductionist view of the totality of exchange, the derived radical politics of which become almost impossible to view. In the struggle to frame his analysis and perhaps find his audience, too, Marx has in other words depoliticized what he just politicized.

Totality or Plurality?

To highlight the significance of the themes I develop in this chapter and compare them with a different kind of reading, consider Harry Cleaver's *Reading "Capital" Politically*. It is an indispensable book for, among other things, being a reading of the first part of *Capital*. But Cleaver argues that in order to grasp the importance of abstract labor, one must skip ahead to the concepts of capital, class, exploitation, etc. and use them appreciatively to reread the first chapter and get its real meaning.[6] This is necessitated, he writes, because

> many interpreters . . . have looked at the determinations of the commodity-form as being abstract characteristics of any and all commodity exchange—from those of a simple or "petty commodity mode of production" to the commodity exchange of capital. In this way the whole analysis of Part I [of *Capital*], including that of exchange in Chapter Two and of money in Chapter Three, has been treated as being separable from the analysis of capital, which is seen as entering only in Part II in "The Transformation of Money into Capital"—as if the money of Part I were either some ahistorical category or that of some precapitalist mode of production.
>
> But the order of Marx's exposition is neither ahistorical nor aimed at reproducing a historical development with the precapitalist-category money preceding the categories of capital.[7]

Cleaver then quotes Marx himself: "It would be inexpedient and wrong therefore, to present the economic categories successively in the order in which they have played the dominant role in history. On the contrary, their order of succession is determined by their mutual relation in modern bourgeois society."[8] Thus, we think the one, real meaning of abstract labor and of value is revealed. Marx develops other strategies in the *Grundrisse*'s chapter on money, however. There (and indeed in the footnotes and asides in *Capital* for which the *Grundrisse*'s preoccupation with utopias was destined), Marx does not need his concept of capital to make his point about abstract/general labor. He already is responding to attempts to address its problems in capitalism—which perhaps is a way of saying that modern bourgeois society is socially complex and bound up with resistances of various kinds, including utopian socialists. Marx's own society, Marx's own political environment, is complex and multiple. If he did not at some level accept this and his analysis of capital completely framed his notion of value (if his notion of value simple reduced to capital), then he would not see how forms such as labor money and time chits would actually be worse than capitalism, as he tells us they are.

A plurality seems to be built into Marx's approach to the question of value and again begs this issue of the perspective from which the value concept views the social field. On what conception of value does the utopian socialist idea of the time chit not work? Is Proudhon wrong because he does not understand how capitalism as value works and thus dooms himself to perpetuating its awful institutions?[9] Or is he wrong because he does not know how to get value as other to capitalism right? Is John Gray's idea for the time chit bank wrong because it would doom us to commodity production? Or is it because he also does not know how to get value right? How to answer these questions is not clear, though Marx's value-in-use makes them possible. If one asks, though, whether what is wrong with the socialist utopians is the same as what is wrong with the commodity form, then the answer is no. They are different systems: the utopian time chit crowd would actually create a worse situation than the one the commodity society already has to deal with. Marx's point about the time chit bank, which performs the service of actually exposing labor time, is that it would make things worse than capitalism and its money basis.[10] This is a curious point because it suggests that capital and value, insofar as it is social labor in search of a form, do not move in lockstep and, in some sense, repel each other. In capital, value cannot appear as what it is.[11] Nor can a full analysis of capital alone put to rest the *question* of what value is. Marx is working up value to be a tool to see precisely what sorts of things go wrong (and right) when labor takes different kinds of social form. The strategy taken, stated as so or not, is that of diverse and interlocking pathways that give the appearance that value is leading different lives in Marx's work and that it is not a determinate thing or even a determinate relation but exists suspended in different kinds and qualities of conversation, debate, and engagement. Consider the three situations that Marx convenes in "The Chapter on Money" and how he evaluates them. When left unplanned, abstract labor cannot work to found a proper political economy. Abstract labor, if it were to be recognized in the form of the time chit, would in fact fail to be recognized. Abstract labor, redefined and reconceptualized, is then placed by Marx at the center of a new economy of qualitative time. But in this proposed new society of associated labor, there is as yet no connective tissue, save for a plan of some kind that would socially adjudicate the different qualities of labor time. Whether such a tissue that is not ideological, not fetishizing, could emerge remains to be seen. (I revisit this question later.) What Marx seems to do here, as he does in part 1 of *Capital*, is to make value a project common to all three situations while not saying they have (a singular) value in common.

Part II

3

The End of Value (As We Know It)

The third volume of *Capital*, like the second, assembled for publication by Engels after Marx's death, is a mammoth tome designed to explore further the themes of the preceding volumes and perhaps to begin the task of integrating them—in flawed and confusing fashion, many have argued. Readers of volume 3 primarily see it as Marx's major statement on how labor values and commodity prices, acknowledged to be different in volume 1 though not dealt with there, are theoretically reconcilable, the former now proved as the basis of the latter. This is the famous transformation problem to which I alluded in the introduction and that is still the subject of debate.[1] Volume 3 of *Capital* is also read as a statement on the inevitability of capitalism's cataclysmic self-induced crisis, intimations of which appear in volumes 1 (oriented toward production) and 2 (oriented toward the circulation of commodities across different departments, or sectors, of the capitalist economy). But this matter, too, of whether capital can perpetually reconstitute itself through crisis and forever stall the Big One, remains contested.

Yet these are not the only concerns we can bring to volume 3. For as Marx explores certain problematic tendencies of value circulation in capitalism he also exposes the richness of his political investments in the value concept. (The tendencies are as follows: that of profit rates to equalize over time, their tendency generally to fall, and the tendency for revenues in capitalist society to be distributed in such a way that the origins of value and surplus value become hopelessly obscured.) But as Marx sets out each of these tendential movements a moment arrives when the specter of associated production erupts on the page, as if in writing about the tendencies of value circulation, Marx was using a pencil with two tips. This is the moment that interests me. Why does it happen and with what pretense? What does this imply about Marx's notion of value? In terms of my method, I am afraid it appears episodic. In no way can I systematically work through the volume. Instead, I quickly zero in on the narrative ruptures where associated production sneaks onto the stage and then try to illuminate those moments for extended study. Such moments could be thought indicative of a haphazard mind, sloppy writing, or maybe bad editing. But they might be indicative of a certain structure of thought, too.

The theme here will be that whereas we might expect value to be about the establishment of the theoretical and conceptual conditions under which we can properly discover the concepts of capital and capitalism, since these concepts do not reveal themselves to us of their own accord, we keep discovering, instead, the specter of associated labor and, thus, a double voice. This specter regularly intrudes on the scene of value. But is it an intrusion at all? How far can we go in reading associated production as the unexpected underlay and warrant of value, right in the heart of capital (a question once posed by Engels)? And does thinking value in capital, through the standard of associated production, contaminate associated production, force it to be thought in certain sorts of ways (a question that I think Engels did not fully foresee)? These questions have to be framed with some care. The idea that associated labor is simply the actual realization of capitalist value, based on transposing capital's accounting of labor time onto socialist arrangements, is a reading of Marx going at least as far back as Engels. Socialism is for him an inversion of capitalism, an inversion that capitalists themselves actively produce as they attempt over time to resolve the very contradictions they produce. For example, because capitalists plan production privately but cannot plan market outcomes, they need to respond in ways that gradually force the socialization of the economy. (As I will point out, Marx indeed makes such observations, though they have more of an experimental air than that of the worked-out totality implied by Engels.) In Jonathan Diskin's words, Engels sees socialism as "always within capitalism as its liberated inner content, trapped in the shell of the fundamental contradiction. The longer capitalism survives, the more fully will it have worked out its social dimensions. But socialism cannot emerge fully within a capitalist society; a moment of transition must exist."[2] Like Engels, I am curious about Marx's investment in a notion of value that is, let's say, stolen from under the foot of capital. But by the end of this chapter and the next, it should be clear that this investment costs Marx something: the discovery of a social limit that cannot be easily overcome, if at all.

In these questions—in Marx's speech as self-interrupting—lay new tidings of value. The plurality of these is, again, what can interest us. What we see when we read Marx on capital is that the prevailing meaning of value (the one we are used to seeing) is outnumbered. To be sure, the dominant meaning—that capital is the maturation and apotheosis of value—gets very, very extended treatment by Marx. But at the level of diversity of concepts and diversity of meaning, something more multivocal takes place.

Strange Tidings in the "Equalization of Profit Rates"

In Marx's view one contradictory outcome of the collective behavior of capitalists is that other things being equal, profit rates across various economic sectors become equalized. This is contradictory because whereas capitalists want to invest in sectors and enterprises that offer higher rates of return on their investments, shifting resources around from lower- to higher-earning enterprises in order to fulfill that want, their doing so en masse and competitively produces the tendency for profit rates to (temporarily) converge. Insofar as this helps to produce a more balanced distribution of resources and revenues, equalization is something like a good thing from a certain value standpoint. I say "something like," since with capitalism we are, after all, talking about a class-based, exploitative system. It is a good thing because what value holds out as a possibility is social evenhandedness. But anything like that, even toward capitalists, is short lived: equalization is merely a mode for the more fundamental disequilibrium and privatization of social power to express itself.[3] Equalization is not Marx's ultimate point, therefore, no matter how many times he refers to it.

In "The Equalization of the General Tate of Profit Through Competition, Market Prices, and Market Value," the final substantive chapter in the part of volume 3 dealing with equalization, Marx establishes for the umpteenth time that the distribution of commodities, of the means of production, and thus of prices and profits necessarily entails a distribution of social labor and social labor time.

> Between the quantity of the article on the market and the market value of this article, there is only this one connection: on a given basis of labor productivity in the sphere of production in question, the production of a particular quantity of this article requires a particular quantity of social labor-time, even though this proportion may be completely different from one sphere of production to another and has no intrinsic connection with the usefulness of the article or the particular character of its use-value. (288)

By extension, if articles produced under these conditions (i.e., commodities) are *bought* by society, then this can be only because "it buys them with a certain quantity of the labor-time it has at its disposal" (288). But "there is no necessary connection"—only a chance one—between how much social labor is spent producing an article, as well as what proportion of the total social labor this represents, and the actual need the article fills. Marx quickly explains the consequences as follows:

> If the commodity in question is produced on a scale that exceeds the social need at the time, a part of the society's labor-time is wasted, and the mass of commodities in question then represents on the market a much smaller quantity of social labor than it actually contains. (288–89)

Then, in the very next sentence, the specter of associated production comes out of nowhere:

> (Only when production is subjected to the genuine, prior control of society will society establish the connection between the amount of social labor-time applied to the production of particular articles, and the scale of the social need to be satisfied by these.) (288–89; parentheses in original)

In a certain reading of *Capital* and its logic, we might expect Marx, at the point where he indicates a problem for capital, to show how it produces yet another side-stepping mechanism, another bourgeois value form. He starts with the idea that labor time is wasted when goods are produced in surplus and then reminds us that value, measured by social labor time, is strictly relative—commodity value does not simply equate with the amount of labor embodied in the commodity but is instead relative to a norm. Thus, commodity detritus starts piling up on one side, and social need, on the other, which is not so good for capital. What should Marx do at this point if he is to remain on task? He now ought to show how value will assume some new, ameliorating configuration. But he does not. He brings a specter onto the stage: a short parenthetical aside through which value as such is simply snatched from the commodity producer's grasp altogether, as well as from the commodity society *tout court*, and given over to its conceptual nemesis, the planned society, or associated labor. That is where value might really happen, insofar as value is itself measured by the balanced distribution of social labor and, thus, of social need. Considering where the reader has been so far, it is a moment to ponder. The concept of value, which in *Capital* has its start in the notion of full compensation for social labor (x amount of linen equals y amount of coats because they share z hours of socially necessary labor time, etc.), gets torn apart and then remodeled on account of all manner of disequilibrating disturbances, only later to be ridiculed as a Sisyphean attempt to secure a form for itself, and seems now to be returned to its premise *even as* that premise is overturned by a different kind of social production. This idea that value's other reality, for Marx, in fact lies outside capitalism is implicitly reinforced as the passage continues.

> If the volume of social labor spent on the production of a certain article corresponds in scale to the social need to be satisfied, so that the amount produced corresponds to the customary measure of reproduction, given an unchanged demand, then the commodity will be sold at its market value. The exchange or sale of commodities at their value is the rational, natural law of the equilibrium between them; this is the basis on which divergences have to be explained, and not the converse, i.e., the law of equilibrium should not be derived from contemplating the divergences. (289)

But what we have just learned is that the sale of commodities at their value as a regularly occurring phenomenon does not actually happen. What is regular is divergence. Divergence cannot be used as a means of discerning the law of equilibrium (i.e., as if equilibrium were just a sort of number hit on by chance). Instead, equilibrium—the balanced connection among labor times—can be established only under associated production. In truth, Marx develops the idea of price of production in an effort to explain how capital attempts to deal in a balanced fashion with differential labor times and unbalanced capital investments. But that is beyond the scope of the discussion here and, I would argue, beside the point. Equilibrium has to be planned out. But by then we're not talking about *commodities* being exchanged at all. "Only when production is subjected to the genuine, prior control of society will society establish the connection between the amount of social labor-time applied to the production of particular articles, and the scale of the social need to be satisfied by these." This statement infects the entire analysis of what value is all about in this chapter. It exposes capitalist value as a blemish, albeit a world-historical one, on the real problem of value by letting us know why value even matters. It lets us know that we again are solving a problem by erasing the conditions that beget the problem. (The discussion of the trinity formula in the following section shows, though, that capitalism does not know what the problem of value even is. Capitalism thinks of a quite different problem—perhaps something like how public virtue comes about through private gain. But *the* problem can be understood only through thinking associated production. Ultimately, this is why associated production bursts onto the stage of Marx's analysis. It seems to be the only way that he can produce the problem for us. He can endlessly analyze capital, but he will never state the problem that way alone. Only these brazen, supplemental insertions can do that.)

Strange Tidings in the "Falling Rate of Profit"

If the falling rate of profit is yet another source of controversy, both in terms of whether profit rates do generally fall and whether such a fall is to be the death knell of capitalism, then it also is another way for Marx to leverage the value concept for purposes of associated production. At the same time, the consequences of such leveraging for associated production become clearer. Marx explains what he means by the "tendential" fall of profit rates within the first few pages of part 3 of volume 3. In essence it involves a secular decline of variable capital in relation to the constant capital. It is "just another expression for the progressive development of the social productivity of labor, which is shown by the way that the growing use of machinery and fixed capital generally enables more raw and ancillary materials to be transformed into products in the same time by the same number of workers, i.e. with less labor" (318). Under these conditions each commodity "contains a smaller sum of labor than at a lower stage of development of production, where the capital laid out on labor stands in a far higher ratio to that laid out on means of production" (318). Collectively, "since the mass of living labor applied continuously declines in relation to the mass of objectified labor that it sets in motion, i.e., the productively consumed means of production, the part of this living labor that is unpaid and objectified in surplus-value must also stand in an ever-decreasing ratio to the value of the total capital applied" (319). Ergo, we have a tendentially falling rate of profit (rate of profit simply being the ratio between the mass of surplus value and the total capital applied). This tendency, Marx stresses, is "*the expression, peculiar to the capitalist mode of production*, of the progressive development of the social productivity of labor" (319; emphasis in original). I think we can take the emphasis Marx lays on this statement in two senses. On the one hand, it is historical: no mode of production developed social productivity as much as capitalism did. On the other hand, the knot of contradictions whose result is the inability of value to take form in capitalism (as opposed to capitalism having developed highly sophisticated means for passing the buck) means that capitalism cannot avoid the falling rate of profit. Nor can it avoid certain of its nasty side effects, such as surpluses of capital, especially means of production, standing cheek by jowl next to surplus populations, a problem that capitalism cannot solve because of the "narrow basis of consumption" (353). That is, means of production are productively consumed for purposes of making a profit, not for meeting social needs. So when means of production stand idle, it's not because social needs have been met.

What is particularly interesting in Marx's discussion of the falling rate of profit—insofar as rising labor productivity is capital's historical role, however ruthlessly played—is his accusation that capital tends to play this role not simply ruthlessly but falteringly, stupidly. This is brought out toward the end of part 3 in two scenarios. In the first, Marx notes that it is primarily new capitals that are motivated by the profit rate. As capital becomes bigger and more centralized (presumably weighed down by its established technological mix) it is the mass of profits that counts more. But since the chase after profit rates is what really animates capital and fuels the historical role of this mode of production, "the animating fire of production would be totally extinguished" if profit rate ceased to be a primary motive (368). Marx notes that David Ricardo fears such a situation but understands neither the underlying forces nor the unintended consequences. Marx writes:

What is visible here [in the tendency toward the centralization and concentration of capital] in a purely economic manner, i.e., from a bourgeois standpoint, within the limits of capitalist understanding, from the standpoint of capitalist production itself, are its barriers, its relativity, the fact that it is not an absolute but only a historical mode of production, corresponding to a specific and limited epoch in the development of material conditions of production. (368)

Marx then offers a second, hypothetical example of how new machinery might not produce a better profit rate than the old. The point is to show that even though capital's general tendency is to increase labor productivity, situations arise in which labor-saving technology is not considered to be a wise choice by capitalists even when the option is there. In the particular scenario given, a new machine is invented that offers significant savings of labor time but depreciates at a faster rate. A capitalist faced with the decision of whether to invest in this new device would decline the option. He would be even more correct to avoid this "utopian stupidity," since it would render his existing machinery worthless before it had even worn out. "For capital, therefore, the law of increased productivity of labor is not unconditionally valid" (371). In all of this, there is now a new contradiction for capitalism. Its historical mission is, for Marx, that it develops labor productivity. But it is "untrue to its mission as soon as it starts to inhibit development of productivity. . . . It thereby shows once more that it is becoming senile and has further outlived its epoch" (371). Marx is showing here in a new way how value, as a process in movement, fails to take form. This process instead must be picked up, carried further, and transformed by associated production.

How value is approached in this scenario involving the labor saving machine is indicative. (Engels puts the entire second scenario in parentheses because according to him, "it goes beyond the original material in certain particulars." See his footnote on page 371.) In fact, the discussion begins with Marx's reminder that "the value of a commodity is determined by the total labor-time contained in it, both past and living" (369). *Past* labor time, we recall, is a determinant of value in the sense that the portion of value of means of production used in the making of a new commodity is passed along during the making. Obviously, *living* labor is involved in the sense that it produces the new commodity. We've seen that the competitive nature of commodity production has a tendency to reduce total labor time, although in truth Marx is keenly aware that this proceeds unevenly in different economic sectors. Moreover, as we've also just seen, a rise in labor productivity does not really count as such if the value passed along through depreciation and/or the use of raw materials is more than or even equivalent to savings in labor time. "The rise in labor productivity consists precisely in the fact that the share of living labor is reduced and that of past labor increased, but in such a way that the total sum of labor contained in the commodity declines; in other words the living labor declines by more than the past labor increases" (369). But in the very middle of this discussion, ostensibly meant to pinpoint the historicity of the value-laden process in capitalism, Marx writes as follows:

> This reduction in the total quantity of labor going into the commodity appears accordingly as the fundamental characteristic of a rise in labor productivity, irrespective of the social condition under which production is carried on. In a society where the producers govern their production by a plan drawn up in advance [i.e., associated production], or even in simple commodity production [i.e., the C . . . M . . . C of part 1, volume 1 of *Capital*], the productivity of labor is in fact invariably measured by such a standard. (370)

So although labor productivity would be assessed by the same measure of time in any society (though, see the following section on the division of revenue), what Marx appears to be saying is that associated production could or would do the job without the distraction of the profit motive, which actually has an inhibiting effect. Just after this passage, Marx describes the predicament of the capitalist who counts as "utopian stupidity" the goal of reducing labor time if this does not serve the first goal of producing profit. And it would also seem to be the case that associated production is not just any sort of producing system: it has a historical role to fulfill, one only falteringly played by capital. That is to say, capitalism cannot live up to its own standards. It instead is hopelessly confused. It engages in a headlong rush to raise productivity only to find itself blocked by its own past investments. ("The barrier to capital is capital itself," Marx writes in part 3.) Capital cannot resolve this tension save through crisis. Just the same, it is precisely the standard of labor productivity upon which associated production must judge its own success, a success it will gain only by overturning commodity production. Nonetheless, associated production proves itself to history and posterity, as it were, by taking on in a clearheaded way the question of value. If in capitalism the development of labor productivity is constrained by the necessity to valorize the existing productive infrastructure (i.e., a constraint imposed by the past), then in the associative scheme to come, the decrease of labor inputs would be a value in itself. And yet just the same, Marx equivocates that the associated producers would not engage in the same headlong, heedless rush to cut labor time (176).

Once again, a major current of Marx's thought—the falling rate of profit, in this case—provides an opportunity to theorize value in capitalism only to turn quite suddenly into the relevance of the value question in planned, associated production. More than just the illusion is given that value in fact belongs to this latter form of production, and at every turn, capitalism is giving up the right to claim this idea as its own. Value no more reduces to capital than capital reduces to value. Capital's development of value is ultimately a false one, a forfeiture, and Marx's theory of capitalism seems to be internal to communal production, which in every regard has capitalistic production surrounded. It cannot be overstated that this is not a theory of historical inevitability. It is a statement concerning Marx's political warrant and remit. It follows on from why he is interested in capital. The starting point of his analysis is not so much the commodity—though Marx says exactly that in his "Notes on Adolf Wagner"—as it is the multiplicity of value, an epistemology through which to know the commodity society and the constraints, qua constraints, that it imposes on itself: a multiplicity carried out in a pattern and rhythm of thought and argument, repeated frequently and that works like a bait and switch. It can always be said that Marx's warrant actually comes from his "scientific" discovery that capital is self-dissolving and does not come from a perspective outside capital, that Marx is simply unveiling a process whose politics are immanent to that unveiling. But it can be replied that for Marx history is open and does not come with guarantees. He and we need reasons to want one sort of future more than another.[4] Value lives on in this way.

Yet this is a difficult moment to sustain. How can capital be contained by something that does not exist at present? It may be saying a lot about thinking with value that the best Marx can do is to hunker down and hypothesize the conditions that capitalism makes possible for its own passing. In the last pages of part 3, he reminds us that when rising labor productivity has its counterpart in the enormous growth of means of production, social power has now become a thing, an independent power in society, far surpassing what "any one particular individual can create" and, from what we've seen, placing regulatory demands on its capitalist functionaries, even while they gain their power from it (373). Because social power exists in a value form—a failed value form—that now far outstrips what individual, immediate producers can accomplish, these producers will be forced to associate. There is no going back to the state of craft production, since the very conditions of production have changed. Marx's point is that the contradictions developed in capitalist society "contain the solution to the situation" that forced individual capitalists to socialize the power of labor in the first place. Capitalists act collectively, though unwittingly, to reify social labor; future associated labor will have no choice but to also act collectively, such are the constraints imposed by an altered means of production. One finishes off this chapter with a sinking feeling, for Marx's analysis is highly consequential. The value process that capitalism has mangled and that

Marx has argued could be done better does not seem to create *its* own solution. For Marx has reminded us powerfully, thrown down the gauntlet really, that people make themselves by making their world materially, and he has stated therein that there are now two time lines to mesh and somehow keep in synch: the time of human becoming and the timing of that becoming by virtue of things. When we invariably produce that by which our productivity would itself be produced, as the passage above would have it, we invariably also reproduce the possibility for these overdetermined times to splinter apart. Does Marx say more than he means before concluding part 3 the way he does? I don't think so. But he does, in his own mise en scene, mirror all too well the value dilemma itself as at once the problem of the mobile norm, the moving standard, and the always-already potential of the material incarnation—of form—to fall short. I have reason in due course to return to this dilemma.

Strange Tidings in the "Division of Revenue"

Marx did not live to finish volume 3; it was Engels's project to get the manuscript into print posthumously. The last great question that Marx undertakes in it—namely, how revenue, including wages and profits, is divided up across the entire terrain of capitalism—covers over half the volume and is split into three major sections and thirty-six chapters. I want to examine only selected portions. The first is a chapter on credit in which Marx describes how credit evolves into a collectivist form of surplus value distribution, with transformative repercussions for both capital and labor. Second is a chapter near the end of the volume on what Marx calls the trinity formula, which considers how all forms of distributed revenue work together to create conditions whereby not only the origins of surplus value are masked but all those involved in its production and distribution perceive no cause to order the world differently. (It is a stunning discussion with reverberations going all the way back to Marx's analysis of the commodity fetish.) Finally, I examine some interesting aspects of a chapter treating how competition specifically acts to disguise the origins of value and surplus value. Consistent with the method proposed in this book, I aim to elucidate not the full content of these discussions but how their digressions teem with implication for the content of the value idea.

Credit: Revolution Commodified

Chapter 27 of volume 3, "The Role of Credit in Capitalist Production," has a narrative arc similar to numerous others of Marx's analyses of capitalist forms. It opens with a concern for such forms and closes with a discussion of a new form of society, that of associated labor. The surprise is that this happens in a chapter on one of the most advanced forms of capital there is, credit, involving a form, money, that is ostensibly anathema to associated production. The chapter begins with a reminder of the various functions that credit has in a capitalist economy. For example, credit is necessary for the equalization of the rate of profit, and it reduces circulation costs (though these functions fit their goals only temporarily and cannot stop the tendency toward crisis). The lion's share of the chapter, a discussion beginning just two pages in, concerns the formation of joint-stock companies, a form of enterprise based upon credit. Such companies allow firms to appear that are larger than could be the case if only a single capitalist were involved. "Capital . . . now receives the form of social capital (capital of directly associated individuals) in contrast to private capital, and its enterprises appear as social enterprises as opposed to private ones. This is the abolition of capital as private property within the confines of the capitalist mode of production" (567). Because profit does not accrue to a single capitalist owner of the firm and its capital stock (i.e., a firm's fixed, constant capital in the form of machinery, factory, etc.), it appears as just what it is, "as simply the appropriation of other people's surplus labor." This is even easier to see given that the formerly "actually functioning capitalist" is transformed into a "mere manager, in charge of other people's capital, and of the capital owner [namely, those other people] into a mere owner, a mere money capitalist" (567). What Marx asserts next is quite surprising, though. He suggests that these changes place the joint-stock company itself in a sort of suspended state such that it is easier to see how its productive operations could be still further ripped from their social context in the commodity society.

> This result of capitalist production in its highest development is a necessary point of transition towards the transformation of capital back into the property of the producers, though no longer as the private property of individual producers, but rather as their property as associated producers, as directly social property. It is furthermore a point of transition towards the transformation of all functions formerly bound up with capital ownership in the reproduction process into simple functions of the associated producers, into social functions. (568)

Yet the "abolition of the capitalist mode of production within the capitalist mode of production itself" is not automatic (569). So Marx pulls back, laying stress on the fact that the command over social labor and social capital afforded by the joint-stock company is all too real. It leads to expropriations of one capitalist at the hands of another, to the formation of huge enterprises, monopolies, pyramid schemes, and swindles. "Expropriation now extends from the immediate producers to the small and medium capitalists themselves. . . . Instead of overcoming the opposition between the character of wealth as something social, and private wealth, this transformation [of wealth in shares] only develops this opposition in a new form" (571).

We then see the continuing significance of the independent form of social power (i.e., money and credit) that emerges out of the value process. But we don't yet see it fully in these passages. For Marx next and immediately draws a contrast with the cooperative factories. These, run by workers, are "within the old form, the first examples of the emergence of a new form, even though they naturally reproduce in all cases, in their present organization, all the defects of the existing system" (571). Marx argues that these cooperatives would not be possible without the capitalist development of the factory system, but also not without the credit system.

The credit system, since it forms the principal basis for the gradual transformation of capitalist private enterprises into the capitalist joint-stock companies, presents in the same way the means for the gradual extension of cooperative enterprises on a more or less national scale. Capitalist joint-stock companies as much as cooperative factories should be viewed as transition forms from the capitalist mode of production to the associated one. (571–72)

Marx therefore concludes that the credit system has a "dual character immanent in it." It develops capitalist production into a colossus of exploitation, gambling, and swindling while simultaneously constituting "the form of transition towards a new mode of production" (572).

If we look back at what Marx makes of labor money and the time chit, we see even further the flexibility of the value concept and the multiplicity of its tropes. In that analysis the only possible way for money to be expressed in a positive manner is for the money function of representing labor to be expressed directly through associated labor. Labor time, as value, cannot be directly expressed at all by the time chit, let alone by money as such. An entirely different form of production would have to be planned, thus in a single stroke addressing the money function by overturning it. Marx takes the utopian socialists to the cleaners on those issues. But here in the analysis of credit, a highly developed form of capitalist money, Marx sees new possibilities for the independent form of social power. If this form of power is truly independent, then it should not matter to its lenders who they sell it to. This is one of the original virtues of money that Marx points out when he begins his analysis in the first part of *Capital*'s volume 1: the disruptive thing about money is that no one needs to know what you're buying with it. The strangest of things and relations can become commodified, and in this way many sorts of social codes can be broken (and new ones implanted). A particular form of value, not the time chit but capitalist money itself, then can be redirected toward building a future society. This produces the very odd paradox that the associated producers of the cooperative factory, in their being associated producers, express the money function by dissolving it (according to Marx's critique of labor money schemes) and at the same time make use of the intact, capitalist money form—of the highest kind, no less.

Radicalizing the Trinity Formula: A Holy Trinity or a Trinity with Holes?

In Marx's analysis of the commodity fetish we saw him argue that the form of appearance of value is such that the question of what value is need not appear and that this process itself allows value to in fact not appear. This theme is renewed in the famous chapter on the trinity formula. The trinity formula refers to three dialectically interwoven factors of production and the forms of income or revenue that accrue to each: capital-profit (including profit of enterprise and interest), labor-wages, and land-rent. Of the total commodity value produced in capitalist society, in other words, a portion goes to capital, a portion to labor, and a portion to landowners. Marx argues that capital's attempt to create value involves so many different forms and transformations of value that average labor time as a common element is moot. In fact, the situation is much more complex and interesting than that. "Disparate as these relations appear [i.e., the different elements of the trinity] they have one thing in common: capital yields the capitalist profit, year in year out; land yields the landowner ground-rent; and labor-power—under normal conditions, and as long as it remains a usable labor-power—yields the worker wages" (960). This is an idea of absolutely crucial importance. Each element of the trinity is in possession of a something that because it can be deployed in its own interests, appears to be the source of revenue for that element. And this appearance, all other things being equal, reappears. It works! More to the point, it functions

without creating the substance itself [i.e., value] that is transformed into these various categories. The distribution rather presupposes this substance as already

present, i.e., the total value of the annual product, which
is nothing more than objectified social labor. But it is not
in this form that the matter presents itself to the agents
of production, the bearers of the various functions of the
production process, but rather in a distorted form. . . .
Capital, landed property, and labor appear to those
agents of production as three separate and independent
sources, and it appears that from these there arise three
different components of the annually produced value
(and hence of the product in which this exists); from
these sources, therefore, there arise not only the different forms of this value as revenues which accrue to
particular factors of the social production process, but
this value itself arises, and with it the substance of these
forms of revenue. (961; emphasis added)

I take this to mean the trinity never has to manifest what makes
it a trinity. It does not have to show what its basis is and does
not have to show itself as totality (i.e., the flux of labor time of
society). And what makes the trinity a trinity works better by
not becoming manifest. No gross product, no sum total, must
be shown around to everyone after it's made and in advance
of its being divided up. That is, once production, circulation,
and consumption are ongoing, the division of the product occurs *simultaneously* with the production of the gross product.
It seems to everyone that nothing, per se, is being divided—
rather, that each and all are merely earning their keep. This is a
brilliant insight. It is enriched by Marx's analysis of how value,
including surplus value, is fragmented into so many forms and
represented by prices that diverge from their basis in value, that
the "threads of the inner connection get more and more lost"
(967). And they seem fated to remain lost given the workings
of everyday life for the actual inhabitants of the trinity formula.

It is . . . quite natural . . . that the actual agents of production themselves feel completely at home in these
estranged and irrational forms of capital-interest,
land-rent, labor-wages, for these are precisely the

configurations of appearance in which they move, and with which they are daily involved. . . . This [trinity] formula also corresponds to the self-interest of the dominant classes, since it preaches the natural necessity and perpetual justification of their sources of income and erects this into a dogma. (969)

Thus, the irrational appears rational because it is the very basis of daily life. It would be irrational to force a change. The irrational indeed is the rational in this scheme of things. Appearances become a force of production.

Marx's only hope as a radical theorist essentially is, here, to fly over the cuckoo's nest and find something rational about the irrational, a rationality that is not simply the appearance of the irrational (i.e., daily life) but something genuinely sensible in itself. That is, he must find something about everyday, daily life that has some other current coursing through it. A point where the idea that things can be much, much different from how capitalism makes them be meets the idea that society in its associated form to come will be doing what societies have always been doing. That is, Marx must in a sense agree that society does not need to change. He must speak of capitalism as irrational and rational at the same time.

In fact, he names this point very early in his analysis of the trinity formula using the same strategy of the abrupt break that we've seen before. In this case, he is in the midst of describing how capital "pumps out a certain specific quantum of surplus labor from the direct producers . . . [and] this surplus labor is expressed in a surplus value, and this surplus-value exists in a surplus product" when he suddenly remarks, "Surplus labor in some form must always remain, as labor beyond the extent of given needs. . . . A certain quantum of surplus labor is required as insurance against accidents and for the progressive extension of the reproduction process that is needed to keep pace with the development of needs and progress of population" (958). (At the end of a later chapter in a similar narrative break, Marx echoes these thoughts, writing that after capitalism is abolished, the "determination of value still prevails."[5]) He is speaking of what needs to be in any mode of production. Marx goes on to remark how capital's "civilizing aspect" of socializing labor and increasing its productivity more than any other historical form, while extorting surplus, is such that it can lead both to the disappearance of the extorting class and to creating "the material means and the nucleus for the relations that permit this surplus labor to be combined, in a higher form of society, with a greater reduction of overall time devoted to material labor" (958). In other words, the first thing that is rational about capitalism is that like any mode of production it organizes human labor and produces a surplus. This is nothing, per se, to be thankful to capitalism for. It is doing what it must. How, then, to take its measure? He writes:

> The real wealth of society and the possibility of a constant expansion of its reproduction process does not depend on the length of the surplus labor but rather on its productivity and on the more or less plentiful conditions of production in which it is performed. The realm of freedom really begins only where labor determined by necessity and external expediency ends: it lies by its very nature beyond the sphere of material production proper. (958–59)

So what capital has done rationally can really be revealed only retroactively, for it is not intrinsically rational. Rationality is a meaning that can be given to the past should capitalism keep producing the future of increased labor productivity and thus possible true freedom. It is a rational system in the narrow sense that it produces a surplus, but the rationality of surplus production in a thicker sense is apparent in the alternative future it opens up. And this future is potentially as fraught as it is revolutionary.

As associated production takes over and transforms the conditions and ends of production it actually expands the realm of needs, of what Marx calls natural necessity. This new desideratum is accommodated, though, because productivity keeps pace: the productive forces are well enough developed to meet the expanded realm of need. Or so Marx wishes. But there are implications for the concept of freedom, which is now subject to equivocation.

> Freedom, in this sphere, can consist only in this, that socialized man, the associated producers, govern the human metabolism with nature in a rational way, bringing it under their collective control instead of being dominated by a blind power; accomplishing it with the least expenditure of energy and in conditions most worthy and appropriate for their human nature. But this always remains a realm of necessity. The true realm of freedom, the development of human powers as an end in itself, begins beyond it, though it can only flourish with this realm of necessity as its basis. The reduction of the working day is the basic prerequisite. (959)

Admirable in this more qualified state of affairs are the rejection of the idea that human nature and human needs are fixed and the implicit corollary that returning to the state of nature, whatever that might be, is not in the offing. We can hear Marx intoning that the human being has changed and will change again. And although it is no doubt difficult for many of us to see Marx wax so optimistic about the human capacity to control interactions with the nonhuman environment, perhaps his rejecting the idea of a return to a state of nature can restore some confidence. The real problems then lie elsewhere. These are, in the very first instance, lodged precisely in the sort of critique Marx engages and the manner by which he goes about it. To wit, in rupturing the narrative of capital (a narrative concerning the capitalist distribution of labor time and commodities, the capitalist penchant to reduce labor time, and the capitalist compulsion to produce surplus), with the specter of associated production, Marx cannot help but to begin describing the various ways that things might go wrong in associated production. These ruptures are, therefore, consequential, being so many knots in which to get tied up.

Recall that Marx's point about the trinity formula is that

capitalism involves an instantiated world of appearances that really are the stuff of daily life. Recall, too, that the discovery of this irrational world prompts the discovery of something rational within it: the simple notion that capitalism shares qualities with other social forms. In this case Marx posits the transhistorical necessity for surplus production. He now has his opening to contrast what this surplus production is like in capitalism versus what it is like in a putative associated production. But we must note that if capitalism, like any mode, must produce surplus, well, so also must associated production. This casts Marx into the difficult terrain of the "real problems" that I suggest lie in wait. These problems lie, I think, in the facility with which Marx approaches freedom and necessity. For starters, if we read the passage closely, Marx takes away the distinction between freedom and necessity only to invoke it again in the next breath: necessity will be experienced as freedom, and freedom will be experienced only beyond necessity. (Though this seems like some regrettably Orwellian double-talk on Marx's part, Sean Sayers very thoroughly traces Hegel's influence on Marx here.)[6] But even that can be worked around if we come up with different words to "really" describe what Marx means beyond his aphoristic proclivity. So the problem is deeper still.

We know that laborers produces their wages (i.e., the value of their wages) and that they also produce a surplus. Marx tells us in volume 1 of *Capital* that the working day is so structured as to disguise the difference between necessary and surplus labor time. Ideology, as described by the trinity formula's world of appearances, consists not only of not being able to see how the differences of time disappear in the working day but also of actually believing in the fullness of appearance. The idea that appearance is *only* appearance goes missing, and this itself becomes reality. How well has Marx pierced through this fabric for the sake of associated producers? Pretty well, but not all the way.

In the passage on freedom, it seems to me that the associated producers are dangerously positioned by Marx to not recognize the difference between need and the realm beyond need. How will the difference be defined? How will it be defined when it is a moving quantum? These are the relatively easy issues, the crass material distinctions between need and beyond-need. Maybe some way can be found to work them out. Much thornier is that the injunction to chart the difference between need and beyond-need is a way of reinscribing work as alienating. Why? Because in placing the true development of human powers outside the realm of necessity, as an end in itself, Marx gives these powers nothing to work on that is essential, that is bound up in need. Put differently, in denying that the realm of need is an end in itself, he belittles it, sullies it, renders it abject. It is a necessary burden.

Thornier still is the world of semblance Marx sets up here. If there is "freedom, in this sphere" of natural necessity, while the true freedom is found in a different sphere, has Marx not concocted an ideology uncomfortably close to what he discovers in the trinity formula? It appears (hah!) that Marx would have the associated producers experience as only a semblance of freedom the very thing they *must* do. Associated producers *must* deal with natural necessity, whereas there is no "must" in the world of true freedom—no gun to the head, as it were—in contrast with what happens if society simply stops producing food or food in certain quantities, for example. The very activities that must happen are ones that at best are semblances of something better. Life can be rich in true freedom, but it *must* be rich in the semblance of freedom. One wants better though, doesn't one? For in Marx's associated production aren't we in some sense still dancing to the beat of the trinity formula? Though it's true Marx writes elsewhere that men start to really produce only once their needs have been met, he has a keen interest in rethinking the very idea of production. Production is the production of life, of society. And we can really start living this out only when the shackles of class oppression and mindless labor abstraction are broken. But we also see here the complications—the return of need, the semblance of freedom versus freedom itself. These complications arise because Marx understands that there are real constraints placed upon any mode of production. Indeed, he says this right up front.

One can see the reasoning here. As Marx complains about the

utopian socialist Charles Fourier, life cannot consist of "mere fun."[7] But neither did Marx want the working day to overtake the day as such. One wants neither all work nor all play. Marx wants to preserve the difference between these two. He is hunting for the right middle ground and the right way to describe the difference. Marx is quite hung up on value here. It seems that he has formulated associated production in value terms—time to be spent on this, time to be spent on that—only to set so many mines to be exploded. In seeking to describe associated production's difference from capitalism in value terms, he has produced the idea of value in an uncanny form, resuscitating what he thought he'd killed. In the passage from volume 3 of *Capital* that I quote several paragraphs earlier, note the easy repetition—"a specific quantum," "a certain quantum"—used to describe surplus in capitalism and in associated production, respectively (958). There is nothing wrong with the basic notion of surplus; Marx names very sensible concerns when he notes that surplus production must be common to every social mode of production. But if in capitalism workers are unable to detect the differentiation of necessary and surplus labor, the associated producers seem similarly poised, left to chart the moving difference between the appearance of freedom ("freedom, in this sphere") and true freedom. Marx fails, it seems, at this point to radically confront and radically name the compulsion to do what *must* be done and seems able to see it only as a degraded form of truth. (If Marx is unable to address this problem, then he would be exactly as Foucault in *The Order of Things* suggests he is, another hack—Adam Smith being another—in the annals of political economy who at the end of the day regards labor as the price we must pay for our existence.)

And there is, finally, an extraordinary problem in having things this way. For this gives the appearance that the form of sociality (social labor) that makes possible the production of what must be produced is itself degraded, not true, not real, not the satisfaction of real desire and real need. (Thus, the seeds are sown to want something different from it.) Moreover, how is production to be organized in the true realm of freedom that exists beyond the production of needs (even expanding needs)?

And is this social production? Personal production? What will make it social production?[8] What will keep personal production and liberal ideas of individuality from reasserting themselves as the desired norm? Add, too, that Marx relegates production for those who cannot work to the realm of necessity. This delightfully bursts the bubble of socialist workers who think they'll get the full proceeds of their labor, but it has the effect of degrading the realm of care to one of obligation and false choice. And if the best solution to these problems is to disguise the difference between "freedom, in this sphere" and true freedom (all is freedom) so that the members of society will be sure to act in the interests of society, then Marx is asking people to misrecognize what he insists is the basis of freedom. Freedom is, like justice, however, one of those concepts that cannot be split up and remain what it is.

The Illusions of Competition and the End of History

Marx's strategy is a risky one. He has just made the argument that (a) because surplus production must be an inherent and necessary aspect of social wealth in any viable society, there is, from this perspective, nothing special about capitalism; and that (b) when he distinguishes between the realm of need and the realm of freedom in associated production, it is less than clear how the realm of need will differ: need seems locked into and trapped by the same generality through which Marx would have led us out of the concept of capital. But of course, he does not resolve everything. It is not in the nature of his writing. He sets too many scenes, throws out too many curves along too many inassimilable trajectories, for such an expectation to be fulfilled. Perhaps, the point is reached where the best he can do is to think value in such a way as to expose the alternate possibilities of historically determinate situations but refrain from specifying too much what value would really look like once it escaped the capitalist condition.

On these terms, what Marx's composing of the value idea does best is, first, return what has become the "dull round of compulsion" to work in the capitalistic way to its politically arbitrary basis, using the value concept to describe, at the same time, capital and its nonnecessity. Examples of this have already been shown. But there is a final example that may help to crystallize the dilemma I discuss earlier in this chapter concerning the contradictions immanent to Marx's method of narrative rupture. It begins with a typical maneuver—the narrative break that with no warning whatsoever, drops a new frame around the analysis of value and shuts out capital. This occurs in chapter 50, the last of the chapters concerning the dividing up of revenue that I treat. The chapter investigates how and why competition (i.e., supply and demand) creates the illusion that the market is what produces profits and accounts for the share of profits taken by different capitalists. Marx's point on this score is, of course, that while value is the source of profits, the equalization of profit rates yields differential prices of production (an allocation of profits to individual capitalists in proportions that don't accord with the surplus value each has produced).

In a long disquisition, Marx explains that value is broken into so many different forms, each appearing to accrue revenue on account of its market position (i.e., the trinity formula), and that there are so many different actors (e.g., industrial and finance capitalists, landowners, workers) whose subject positions within capitalism are reproduced by their own actions—these actions being perceived as based on the forms of appearance of capital (e.g., the trinity formula, again)—that market competition appears to be the ultimate arbiter in dividing up total revenue. Once commodities have actually been made, that is, it appears that the market is an independent *causal* force in differentially distributing the rewards. Marx wants to say, rather, that competition is a mechanism that allows the actual cause to operate obscurely. In addition, though, the illusory powers of competition arise from the engrained way in which bourgeois economy comes to think itself. The revenue forms of wages, profit, and land rent become so reified to the bourgeois economist "that this method [of analysis] is used even where the conditions of existence for these forms of revenue are completely lacking. . . . That is to say, everything is subsumed under them, by way of analogy" (1015). Bourgeois political economy puts capitalist production into a synecdochal and reified relation to production as such: all production looks like bourgeois production. Thus, "if an independent worker [for example, a peasant] labors for himself and sells his own product . . . he is first of all considered as his own employer, employing himself as a worker, and as his own landowner, using himself as his own farmer. He pays himself wages as a worker, lays claim to profit as a capitalist and pays himself rent as a landlord" (1015). The problem is that this analogy does not help us understand the basis for distinguishing between peasantry and capitalism as distinctive modes of production, even though "revenue" circulates in each type. "Because a form of production that does not correspond to the capitalist mode of production can be subsumed under its forms of revenue (and up to a certain point this is not incorrect), the illusion that capitalist relationships are the natural condition of any mode of production is further reinforced" (1015).

Now comes the characteristic break, the sting. Can we not recode or break apart capital's own categories in order to *dissolve* its historical specificity ("up to a certain point this is not incorrect"!) and open up an aleatory space in which to think both it and something beyond it? Apparently, we can.

> If . . . wages are reduced to their general basis, i.e., that portion of the product of his labor which goes into the worker's own individual consumption; if this share is freed from its capitalist limit and expanded to the scale of consumption that is both permitted by the existing social productivity (i.e., the social productivity of his own labor as genuinely social labor) and required for the full development of individuality; if surplus labor and surplus product are also reduced, to the degree needed under the given conditions of production, on the one hand to form an insurance and reserve fund, on the other hand for the constant expansion of reproduction in the degree determined by social need; if, finally (1) the necessary labor and (2) the surplus labor are taken to include the amount of labor that those capable of work must always

perform for those members of society not yet capable
or no longer capable of working—i.e., if both wages and
surplus-value are stripped of their specifically capitalist
character—then *nothing of these forms remains, but
simply those foundations for the forms that are common to all social modes of production.* (1015–16; emphasis added)

In other words, why must capitalism's forms be the ones anointed
for founding political economy? Indeed, they don't have to be.
For many readers of Marx, everything rests on the idea that
Marx is at all times a *historical* thinker of capitalism, only ever
describing it and theorizing it in ways that show its historical
specificity at every point within its marrow.[9] But he is as capable of dehistoricizing it or, at least, of having his way with
historicization so that time itself can be returned to its openness, its decidability. To what advantage? Well, here everything
depends on our ability to substitute an understanding of essential events and processes that take place in capitalism with an
understanding of what must happen anyway. While I discuss
an example similar to this in the previous section, this iteration
contains certain special effects worth pointing out. Capitalism
is deprived not only of its specialness, its privilege, but also of
playing the synecdochal part to the whole of economic forms. In
fact, Marx reverses the situation. Just as bourgeois economy re-
writes other forms of production as its own, erasing their social
and historical specificity, Marx erases capital's, writing over its
specificity with his own transformative concepts. It could be argued that he has all the more emphasized capital's historicity, as
if to say capital's own historical position is that it cannot make
the necessary distinctions between one type of production and
another. But this is not, in the end, terribly helpful. And I don't
think it is correct, either. Marx is searching gamely, insistently,
and repeatedly for a way to get us out of a particular trap. He
needs to show not simply the historicity of everything but the
contingent nature of that historicity: necessity and nonnecessity at the same time.
  The particular way he does this resembles, of course, what I

discuss in the previous section, on the commonality of surplus production to all viable modes of production, but perhaps with some added, more comprehensive force. The message here is that to see in events and processes necessity and nonnecessity at the same time is to accept both the reality on the ground and the different reality that might also have been and could be. This isn't just a way of seeing, of naming; it's not simply about nomenclature. Things really could be otherwise. There was and is always and already the possibility of this otherness. To use Marx's words, "foundations" are real at the same time as specific "forms" are real. When things change, they must have already had the potential to be otherwise. And if things are going to change, there isn't just one way for them to go. Recall Marx's comment on the corrected form of the time chit bank: it would be either a dictatorship of production or production under common control. Recall his analysis of credit and its intrinsic duality. There is something radically nonidentitarian in this. Processes, events, and things are not in possession of themselves. They instead remain *possessed by* the field of possibility from which they emerge and which itself never loses its reality. But let's not confuse things with such a thought, either. This is still a world where most things don't change overnight and where some things may well nigh be impossible. And more to the point, Marx is primarily interested in the particular directions contingency might go, arguing that the capitalist production of surplus—how this happened—is specifically useful for its abolition by associated production.

In finding a limit to how capital knows itself and would itself insist on being known, Marx opens up a space of possibility and choice for us. The space is most convincing to the extent he can convince us that it is precisely the forms capital invents to do what any mode of production must do that screw things up and destabilize production, turning what must be into progressive catastrophe—in all senses. The space is less convincing to the extent that as I try to show, Marx invokes a set of determinations that are themselves clouded. That is to say, he does more than simply show us the foundations of production; he deals in forms of a kind. And he seems not to notice this as well as he might. But he cannot do everything, and he does a lot—as each of the narrative breaks and strange tidings explored in this chapter evince. The space of possibility is not pure and absolute and is always borne from within whatever the impure space of present potentials has to offer. Possibility has inbuilt proscriptions. Is this a fatal condition?

Conclusion

Volume 3 of *Capital*, designed, among other things, to draw out the tendencies of the circulation of value in capitalism, also is nothing other than an opportunity for Marx to point out other strange tidings, a life of value beyond capital. Thus, the discussion of the equalization of profit rates seems to demand, for a thinking of the very problem it is, recourse to a conception of value outside capital. That is easily enough said and a nice echo of ideas found in the first chapters of *Capital*, volume 1, and "The Chapter on Money" in the *Grundrisse*. The falling rate of profit thesis hints, however, that the inheritance of the dead labor (the vast labor-saving materiel of capital) will compel a determinate form of associated production, devolving into a tendency to force a certain kind of collectivization of labor modeled by the collectivity of capital. Marx therefore does not think himself free to denote the lives of value in any way whatsoever; unlike in *Capital*, volume 1, these lives may be connected and mutually determining. But he does not seem to like such constraints very much. Future value must be radically free—the division of revenues, where Marx inserts his thinking about the simultaneous necessity and nonnecessity (or the rationality and irrationality) of capitalism, and the absolute difference between free and necessary production are stamped by a little utopianizing of his own.

With these narrative breaks, with each movement of a pawn in the game of value's telling, Marx has not reached the last rank of the chessboard, retrieved his queen, and produced a checkmate, a final, uncontested showing of what value *really* is. He has instead prolonged the game.

4

From Necessity to Freedom
and Back Again

Abjected Labor, Tainted Value

Is Value Necessary in Capitalism?

No. But also, yes! Sort of. Repeatedly, Marx shows that value is a problem that eludes capital's apparatuses. In showing us that capital is a failed attempt to give determinate shape and form to value, he shows that value, in an alternate reckoning, lies elsewhere, in a world that remains to be made. It is a very risky strategy, as I have suggested, for the more he repeats his point, leveraging this, that, and the other mechanism or outcome of capital to do so, the more he conjures a set of problems whose solutions are hardly automatic or self-evident. Indeed, it is fair to say that he is producing a problem much more than a solution. Because the problem hinges so much around Marx's strategy of positing capitalism's specificity *together with* its generality, I would like to venture some thoughts about this ensemble of the specific and the general, ultimately to return to the problem of freedom and necessity in associated production, to which it is so intimately related.

The usual way of dealing with the notion of general production and Marx's invocation of it is to say it is a conceptual abstraction, a means of making some fairly simple comparisons and contrasts after which we move on to the preferred emphasis on historically and socially specific forms of production. Another meaning, already seen, is to equate it with the idea of expenditure of labor time, regardless of particular objective. I would like to try a different approach, however, and suggest that the idea of production in general is the idea of what society, any society, must be capable of doing. This is to say a people must produce its life, and its life will be, other things being equal, the consequence, intended or not, of what it does. Capital cannot simply do what it wants; it must accommodate itself to the general production that operates within it, in the scene just noted, just as this generality cannot operate or exist by itself independently. I am not saying, therefore, that production in general has an independent existence but that rather a certain kind of production must be done that produces and reproduces society as such. (One could say that general production is a specific kind of production, after all—that is, that the other side of general production as potentiality is that potentiality is restricted.) If we really grasp the demands of general production, then we can garner further insight into the *functioning* failure, so to speak, of value, or what I earlier denote as the improbability of value, in capital: the recurring nonoccurrence of value in capital (for example, that prices diverge from value poses value as something that continually departs from and chases after its own forms). But as this is a very abstract point, let me pose a concrete question to which it gives rise: *When value fails to appear and yet is the essence of capital, why doesn't life in capitalism always-already come to a crashing halt?* Surely this is the question to have in mind when setting out to explore the putative necessity of value in capitalism, capitalism's failure to meet this requirement, and yet also the general production that shines through. This is an exploration that has everything to do with the actual presence of the potential for alternatives to capitalism. Cesare Casarino puts this exceptionally well: "The common is virtually indistinguishable from that which continually captures it, namely capital," for the reason that capital and the common each has its existence in the one and only surplus, life as a living potentiality.[1] If I branch off from Casarino's arguments, though, it is in the view that Marx's passage through value theory is rich with implication for thinkers of the common (i.e., life as living potentiality). As I increasingly argue toward the end of this book, the value-theoretic mode cannot be laid aside in favor of the concept of the common, as if a politics of the common would resolve the politics of capital (value). Value is, I think, prophetic for the common. As Jason Read observes, though without reference to value, a problem for the common is that it will always have "forms of appearance" and will always tempt us to regard the common as identical to its forms.[2]

Parsing the necessity (or not) of value would seem hardest to do in the very place where Marx thinks value as law—the law of value. In the chapter "Relations of Distribution and Relations of Production," again from volume 3 of *Capital*, Marx writes that this law is an "inner law."[3]

> The product as commodity and the commodity as capi-talistically produced commodity give rise to the entire determination of value and regulation of the total produc-tion by value. In this quite specific form of value labor is valid only as social labor; on the other hand the division of this social labor and the reciprocal complementar-ity or metabolism of its products [that is, commodity exchange where by the value of one commodity gets expressed only by a different commodity], subjugation and insertion into the social mechanism [presumably, successful market exchange and consumption], is left to the accidental and reciprocally countervailing mo-tives of the individual capitalist producers. Since these confront one another only as commodity owners, each trying to sell his commodity as dear as possible, . . . *the inner law operates only by way of their competition, their reciprocal pressure on one another,* which is how divergences are mutually counterbalanced. It is only as an inner law, a blind natural force vis-à-vis the individual agents, that the law of value operates here and that the social balance of production is asserted in the midst of accidental fluctuations. (1020; emphasis added)

Without saying so in precise terms, Marx is, I think, harking back to the retroactive, *a posteriori* quality of value: value is only value when a certain process has completed itself. Indeed, he is saying precisely this but in a different way (although, as I hope I have emphasized enough, this process never *truly* completes itself). Value emerges as a consequence of capitalists confronting each other. It concerns the results of their actions and the ceaseless confrontation with those results. The law of value therefore is not something that preexists these actions but has its existence only within them. The law of value is an immanent law, in other words. (Marx refers to the origins of capitalism in volume 1, in similar terms, as arising "spontaneously"—that is, not out of nothing and not imposed from some outside but through mutual interactions.)[4] At the same time, because these capitalists confront each other not as planners in common but as private owners of commodities to be gotten rid of on a competitive, profit-seeking basis, they are going to act only in certain restricted ways. But if value is taken as a consequence and as a continuing confrontation with consequence, then these consequences must be taken as dynamic and changing, and tendential. The ways in which such confrontations can unfold are constrained by the given range of social positions available. As seen in volume 3, for example, they involve an increase of constant capital (dead labor) as against the decreasing need for labor power (living labor) to put a given constant capital to work.[5] This is not thought ahead at the historical origins of capitalism but is one of the results of value, of consequent actions patterned after consequent actions, repeatedly escaping the forms invented for them and seeking others, there never being just the right way to dispose of commodities or the perfectly advantageous way to model production.

What does this mean for the question in front of us? Value (in the trope deployed here) is not a necessity; it's a consequence. There *is* a necessity for capitalists to orchestrate their attempts at value production in restricted sorts of ways, but this necessity is also an inner one reflecting the position and possessions of capitalists. On this basis, then, it seems to me that capitalism need not produce value at all. What happens instead is a semiorganized, semichaotic *effort to keep up with or undercut* prevailing norms of labor time and, in consequence of this, an avalanche of forms out of balance, a piling up of consequence and crisis. It is deferral all the way up and all the way down. But is it necessity of value? No. And yet how can it be possible, having just now parsed the nonnecessity of value (or, if you like, necessity read as consequence and ceaseless, endlessly failing encounters with consequence), that production in general, the thing that must be done, still shines through? It seems I have betrayed the very notion of production in general that I have been singling out for importance, if value cannot account for it, and I have betrayed value as the essence of capital if I am saying it need not be produced. Where exactly does the production that must be done exist?

Marx already parses out an answer (I admit the question itself is a coy one) when he writes in his critique of labor money that solving the problem of money demands a grasp of what really is already happening in society: production as a general phenomenon. And he does so when he calls the bluff of dehistoricized political economy: forms of life in capitalism can be returned to a basis common to all production. And he does so when he anatomizes the trinity formula, too: value cannot be except that production has already happened, and yet production's having already happened does not manifest (make self-evident) value. What do these scenarios convey in common? By the time something called value has (not) happened, daily life is always-already being lived. What does this mean? It means that value in capitalism never has to see that capitalism, whatever else it might be, implies production in general. The retroactive quality of value allows all manner of departures from ostensibly equivalent value metamorphoses without daily life coming to a crashing halt. It is not just the workings of the market, then, that allows for prices to diverge from value but witless production itself. Note well that this argument does not necessitate celebrating daily life in capitalism. The many problems with need fulfillment, poverty, and misery in capitalism that Marx explores in *Capital* and elsewhere are well known. But Marx specifically discounts struggles over wages and unemployment as quite beside the point in the struggle against capitalist value (see volume 1 of *Capital*). I believe Marx is saying that we better understand what value is about when we discount or bracket off immiseration. That is, we need to be able to grasp value's distinctiveness as a concept *even if* the quality of life under capitalism is in some material sense improving. This is not to deny that the process of chasing down value does not ever create a precarious existence, but it is to say that the problem of value continues apace even when the standard of living rises.

Some paragraphs earlier, I state that capital cannot simply do what it wants; it must accommodate itself to the generality that operates within it. From the standpoint of value, this accommodation happens in a negative rather than an affirmative way. What Marx is describing *is a society that does what must be done without ever bringing this requirement to consciousness.* It is a society whose needs are met (other things being equal) chaotically and through division without ever being summed up ahead of time, brought into view, and then consciously divided. (Obviously, the solution is not planned commodity production, as should be clear from prior discussions [e.g., labor money].) Instead, as the trinity formula suggests, only the fragments appear, not the social substance that binds them. What we are now getting the sense of, through the concept of general production, is why these appearances and the actions they predicate can become real. *They can become real because they effect the general (doing what must be done) at the same time as they are specific (specific to capitalism).* In no way is this an argument through the back door for capitalism or a failure to recognize the immiseration toward which capital tends, just as the different examples of slavery or feudalism would not be an argument for slavery or feudalism. It instead is a statement only of what a human society must be capable of doing and, for Marx, the worthwhileness of producing human society consciously and in a direction that increases human emancipation and productive powers. It is a statement that says we understand an important strain of Marx's outlook on capital when we see it—and I use this term advisedly—working. Focusing on the perception that capital supports us reveals something that is hard to see when we perceive only exploitation. (In this sense, Moishe Postone is right to argue that Marx is overvalued as a theorist of exploitation and underappreciated as a theorist of how society and history are posited and produced in capitalism.)[6]

Let me venture the following, then: that the anarchic progression of appearances made real has its basis not simply in the social relations of capitalism but in capitalism as particular and general at the same time and that value (in the usual sense) need not be produced at all, value being a concatenation of endless deferrals, and yet production in general must be produced. The latter postulate says that the implicit priority usually attributed to the specific over the general is disrupted. Value (in the usual sense) is saved from extinction by production in general, which makes possible value's paradox, that it (value) is possible to not be possible. Put differently, production in general is always-already there; value's job (in the usual sense) is to repress it. But the joke ultimately is on value. (In the passage on the law of value, note that Marx makes a distinction between product and commodity right off the bat. Before things in capitalism are commodities, they are products.) Therefore, is it too much to say that if production in general is a necessary (though insufficient) condition for the birth of capitalism as a historical form, then it also is a condition within capitalism, providing for the capacity for value to race from form to form while never quite spelling the end of daily life? The race of value from form to form ("as the hart pants after fresh water") is undergirded by production in general, value in another key. Value is abstract labor, on the one hand, and general production, on the other.

This business of production in general is double edged, however, as Marx notes. It must have relevance to capitalism *and* to associated production. On the one side, by virtue of production in general, capitalism is toppled from its synecdochal position. Seeing capitalism as production in general is to also see that specific production and consumption arrangements could be otherwise. The trinity formula shows how daily life in capitalism is constituted of a world of appearances whose truth need never manifest. I argue earlier that what Marx does is to radicalize this irrationality by finding something rational within it, a something that is also being produced. This rationality, production in general, which grounds the possibility of a new emancipated and emancipating social form, is the companionate truth of capital, but whether this truth does make an emancipatory turn is not an inevitability. At the same time, its reality as a possibility exists thanks to the generality of production that also defines capitalism. On its other edge, production in general shows us what associated production must also be capable of doing; it must among other things produce a surplus. In his handling of this issue, Marx parses associated production as a certain relation between necessity and freedom. I have already gone on at length about what I perceive to be the problems with how he poses this relation and in a moment will return to these, but what do I hope to have done by way of the value concept in Marx?

This is all about trying to secure an argument for how value can be at once historically and socially specific and have application and relevance transhistorically—and making this argument in the terms Marx gives us. I have said that value is in some sense ontologically enabled by not having to see the production in general that always precedes it and always accompanies it. What this allows us to see more clearly perhaps is that in Marx's analysis the concept of value in the commodity society is a concept of the limit points where social power (the being and becoming of social labor) fails to gain representation but does not itself fail. The ultimate such point is the failed expression of value in money, the object par excellence in which social power is by turns embraced and turned away. In the commodity society value *is* not having to bring to consciousness the social power that is produced and the manner whereby this happens; it *is*, by inner law, the making of the social substance without manifestation of social substance. Value therefore *is* doomed to outstrip and fall short of social power. It outstrips social power in the sense that existing social powers are never sufficient to what this value requires and it falls short in the sense that social power predicates value and constitutes what else it might be. Value in this formulation is a social way of not seeing and not having to see what happens in capitalism. In short, value in commodity society is fucked-up necessity. Then, via associated production, Marx suggests solving the problem of value, or I should say, *reviving it properly*, by bringing what he calls the realms of necessity and freedom to consciousness and into balance.[7] Necessity and freedom are, as I imply earlier, highly fraught divisions of social power but nonetheless involve a distinction that Marx finds useful when arguing that in associated production social power will always be in the place(s) it needs to be, distributed in the proper proportions in an ongoing fashion.

Rethinking Necessity

There may be many problems left unsolved and unstated up to this point, but the one that I find most perplexing and unsettling, as Marx works toward a depiction of associated labor, is that the realm of necessity, that which must be done, is rendered by him in abject terms, excluded from the realm of real desire and freedom. As such, he threatens to reinstate social labor on unemancipated ground. The question is, it seems, how to render such a realm in terms of desire and freedom. How can one come to see what must be done in terms of a choice? How can the paradox of *choosing* to do what *must* be done be resolved? How can we free up the idea of labor determined by necessity so that necessity is in some sense freely chosen? Right off the bat, this is a very risky question for anyone proposing to read Marx's texts with their grain. Marx is less interested in plotting out choices than social roles, relations, conditions, immanent becomings, and movements. Yet let's not fool ourselves; he is in the business of trying to persuade us that a fetishized existence along the axes of the trinity formula is no real existence and that when capitalism fails it would be better to associate of our own accord than be forced or prodded into it by despotic rule. Marx is not a believer in the inevitability of specific historical changes. Time won't rescue us; we'll still have to produce it. Somewhere along the line, people must come to believe that one way is better than another or at least worth trying out.

I would like to approach the issue counterintuitively by looking at what happens when a choice is made to give up necessary production. In other words, how do matters look when the *choice* is made to *not* produce needs or to reduce them or to dial back one's active participation in the realm of needs? What does

Marx have to say about this? As it happens, a lot. In fact, there is a series of illustrative figures to be excavated from Marx's texts that are ready grist for the question. Recall that in his preliminary exploration of how individuals in the commodity society, considered as simple circulation (C . . . M . . . C), could accumulate surplus, even while predicating their affairs on the exchange of equivalents, Marx offers the figure of the miser (hoarder). The miser voluntarily undergoes self-deprivation in order to accumulate wealth: C . . . M . . . c(m) . . . C . . . M . . . c(m′) . . . C . . . M . . . c(M) . . . C . . . M . . . c(M′) . . . . In shortchanging himself, the miser lays a trap, however. He is haunted by the needs that he refuses to increase and by the ones that he used to fulfill for himself. As seen earlier in the initial discussion of the miser, this figure is haunted by what Marx—following Aristotle—describes as "this contradiction between the quantitative limitation and the qualitative lack of limitation of money."[8] And as an owner of social wealth turned private hoard (m . . . m′ . . . M . . . M′), he is in possession of a social substance (money) that cannot be what *it* is, because it's been ripped out of the social sphere, where it wants to be. Because the miser withdraws money from circulation, he displays this social power in a stunted form. Thus, the miser shortchanges himself twice. To be a miser is to be mad with pent-up social energies and desires that seek some sort of escape.

But in the relation between capital and labor, the miser appears to find the perfect solution to his misery. It is perfect (in appearance) because now, as a capitalist, he gets to inhabit just the one side, capital, the realm of freedom, while devolving the realm of necessity to the laborer. As a capitalist, he circulates money *and* amasses wealth *and* develops the capacities of social labor. It appears that M becomes M′ through no cost to himself: labor is assigned to the laboring class, upon whom the miser's asceticism is now foisted.[9] Thus arrives the formula for expanded circulation: M . . . C . . . M′. But this is a mere appearance. For Marx argues that in carrying his power in his pocket, the capitalist deprives himself of the chance to develop essential aspects of his own being. The social power he wields is no essential aspect of *his own being.* Such a being can only be won through direct interaction with nature, which as explained in the chapter on money in the *Grundrisse* (and in earlier works, such as *The Economic and Philosophic Manuscripts of 1844*), is synonymous with the development of real human individuality, whereas the "possession of [money] is not the development of any particular essential aspect of his individuality."[10] The capitalist's and the miser's coin are, in fact, the same; they just express opposing sides. The miser actively deprives himself of the objects, of the fruits and benefits, of his work; the capitalist forfeits the chance to essentially develop himself. The wealth of the capitalist is not real wealth at all, only another expression of self-deprivation and self-denial. Marx indicates, too, that the capitalist is forever scrutinizing his own consumption, anyway, as he searches to balance contradictory impulses to plow money back into production for profit, to spend on himself, and to spend for the sake of displaying his wealth as the good capitalist should. Capitalism then is all around a system in which it is impossible to not self-deny. Marx makes much of the farcical results: capitalist and laborer each suffer, and yet social power, per se, is mounting all around. (By the time he develops his concept of modern industry in the first volume of *Capital*, the farce is potentially revolutionary. Capital's negation of labor's development multiplies so radically—through substitutions of machinery for labor power and the subordination of labor to machinery across so many sectors of production—that Marx sees the makings of a new kind of worker, one suddenly more well-rounded than before because she is able to span a wider portion of the social division of labor. As in mathematics, so in capitalist production: the multiplication of negatives produces a positive.) How does all of this bear on the question, now, of choosing to do what must be done? It asks that we reconsider what this injunction of "must" is all about. In consideration of these figures of the miser, the capitalist, and the laborer, it appears Marx has altered the notion of necessity. What must be done can instead be seen as what is essential to do in order for essential aspects of our being to develop.

After capitalism, though, what would these workers do to free themselves? The implications of all of this are not as clear as they might seem. In an alternative society, would workers simply reverse the terms established by capital and keep the fruits of their labor for themselves? Marx warns against exactly that sort of politics of exploitation in the *Critique of the Gotha Program*. The fruits of labor are in no way immediate possessions of workers; they are mediated possessions, instead, because there is still a wider realm of need to be addressed: care for those who cannot yet or no longer can work, shoring up provisions for the future, diverting resources toward production of new means of production. All such things must be accounted for, and well, it appears the starting point has reemerged: the realm of need is not the realm of freedom, just as Marx writes (and just as Foucault writes of Marx). But the virtue of excavating and thinking through this chain is to show that it is possible to arrive at the starting point from a perspective different from Marx simply throwing down the gauntlet, for we now have the means to discover how *not* to express our desire for the realm of freedom and the enjoyment of material wealth and why it is desirable to choose to produce in the realm of need.

The figurative series is in some sense a choice set, history being unguaranteed and uncertain. It is politically necessary for Marx to extinguish our desire to move backward along the proverbial chain in a quest for freedom. He must show that when the production of needs is forfeited or pawned off on someone else, something is lost. The realm of need, of producing needs, because it's a realm involving the discovery and production of essential being, ought to be desired and chosen in itself. Just the same, it is marked by a kind of intentionality, even a functionality, that does not serve the fuller sense of freedom that Marx seems to be holding out for us. Therefore, I want to explore the possibility of a more positive grounding for freedom in this realm of necessity. It seems to me that founding the freedom Marx desires by exploring the negative case of what it costs us to forsake production goes only so far. For the Marx seen here is the Marx who famously distinguishes humans from other animals by the fact that they have the capacity to construct first in imagination what they then intend to build on the ground: this is what makes the difference between the "worst of architects" and the "best of bees."[11] We have an idea of what to make; we have the know-how to make it; and when we are done making it, we have produced not just the thing but ourselves, as well. This virtuous circle is good so far as it goes. The problem is it lacks surprise. It is wanting in serendipity. It is a little boring and self-satisfied. But in reading Marx, there *always* is something a little surprising around the corner, so much did he write and in so many ways did he experiment with writing what he wanted to write. Which is to say, another analysis is ready at hand of how Marx sees the labor process and what it is capable of producing by way of essential being. Around the middle of *Capital*, volume 1, Marx begins a lengthy and quite extraordinary series of chapters on changes in the labor and production process since the birth of capitalism and on through his own day. Except for the fact that it is a continuation of his analysis of the commodity and of value, it is like a self-contained book within the larger book. The first chapter in the series, like the first chapter of *Capital* itself, is the pacesetter. Marx begins with an immanent or spontaneous definition of capital's origins. Capitalism really appears once large numbers of wage workers are assembled under the auspices of capital.[12] It is something of a tautology, but it once again tells us that capitalism's laws are inner laws, that Marx here thinks of capitalism as a historical form (though see my previous discussion), not a form given at the beginning of time. If so, what is labor like under these conditions? It above all is what Marx describes as a cooperative form of labor. It involves workers working side by side. This changes everything. For one, labor becomes more productive, the value of individual commodities consequently falls, and a number of other effects on capital value follow in train, which do not need to be reviewed here. But Marx also makes much of the effects on laboring itself when "numerous workers work together side by side" (443). "Not only do we have here an increase in the productive power of the individual, by means of co-operation, but the creation of a new productive power, which intrinsically is a collective one" (443). This power is not just a number or a quantum of productive force; it is rendered as a qualitatively different experience.

Apart from the new power that arises from the fusion of many forces into a single force, mere social contact begets in most industries a rivalry and a stimulation of the "animal spirits," which heightens the efficiency of each individual worker. . . . This originates from the fact that man, if not as Aristotle thought a political animal, is at all events a social animal. (443–44)

Marx revels in the sociality of this animal, seeing it even as a different kind of animal: "a body of men working together have hands and eyes both in front and behind, and can be said to be to a certain extent omnipresent" (445). In contradistinction to when an individual works alone, producing some article in a series of sequential acts, "the various parts of the product come to fruition simultaneously" (445). Cooperation is the "social productive power of labor, or the productive power of social labor. This power arises from co-operation itself. When the worker cooperates in a planned way with others, he strips off the fetters of his individuality, and develops the capabilities of his species" (447). It is true that in capitalism workers do not come together to produce commodities cooperatively unless capitalists bring them together. For this reason it appears as though it is capital's power that produces this augmented productivity. "Because this power costs capital nothing, while on the other hand it is not developed by the worker until his labor itself belongs to capital, it appears as a power which capital possesses by its nature—a productive power inherent in capital" (451). But against this apparent power of capital, capital merely appropriates this form of social power. The social power itself is a property of cooperative labor as such: pure surplus. As Marx digs further into the labor process, chasing down its history from simple cooperative forms of labor on through successive chapters on manufacturing and machine-based modern industry, we find him describing the subversion and distortion of cooperation. But it is never extinguished once and for all and, like general production, shines through. Cooperation "remains the fundamental form of the capitalist mode of production, although in its simple shape it continues to appear as one particular form alongside the more developed ones" (454).

There are some very useful ideas in these passages. We humans are not social beings before acting socially: our sociality is a potential that has to be actualized. You might plan for it, but it does not exist in the plan per se. And when we work together, we are more than the sum of our individual parts; such fetters fall away. Marx describes the unleashing of "animal spirits" and an atmosphere of "emulation." We find ourselves enlivened, spurred on, desirous of remaining in this mix. It seems to me that Marx is alerting us to the unplanned effects of even planned work (work planned by capitalists), that he toys with an idea of humanity quite different from that invested in the notion of the "worst of architects." We are the species that can surprise itself. As Cesare Casarino argues in a marvelous study of Herman Melville's *Moby Dick*, Marx also seems to suggest that our experience of ourselves is dispersed throughout the now collective body. We find ourselves not in ourselves but in and through the bodies of others. What fringe benefits! A new being results with eyes on all sides of its head. One can say that Marx here views the realm of production through rose-colored lenses. And maybe (certainly) he is. But what sense is there in denying the ample evidence that people have the capacity to experience extraordinary joy and pleasure in working with each other simply because they are working together: the giddy sensation that one is smaller than what one thought (a part of a whole) and larger than what one is (stripped of individual fetters), that one has become folded, along with others, into a new creature altogether.

Marx's arguments in these chapters have an affinity with some similar but I think less developed points in the *Grundrisse*. In that work Marx argues that although labor is, on the one hand, a response to "merely natural urgencies" (i.e., humans must produce in order to live), on the other hand, once laboring, the individual is in the act of positing himself. Labor becomes "posited as aims which the individual himself posits—hence as self realization, objectification of the subject, hence real freedom, whose action is, precisely, labor" (611). He goes on to write that such a positing cannot happen until labor becomes truly social (i.e., associated, etc.). But again, this "real freedom" is trumped, problematically, by the freedom that begins after the work of meeting material needs is done. These and the reflections of the past few pages seem to me useful for returning more productively to the quandary Marx leaves us in when elsewhere dividing the realms of freedom and necessity. The point of the potential pleasures I describe is that *they are not reducible to the labor that brings them about*, as if the ideological side of a good work ethic. By the same token, they do not exceed labor; they are not cut off from it—they are not imbued with magical powers independently capable of transforming all situations. What Marx has done is give us a way to think that choosing to do what must be done can be in the act of doing itself, not even preexisting it but subsisting immanently within it. In this sense, then, *the realm of necessity need not be regarded as simply an effect or epiphenomenon of the realm of freedom*. It has qualities of its own. To be experienced as pleasure, cooperative acts do not require us to regard labor abjectly. What these points all have in common is that this mode of work is a realm of unintended consequences, surplus, and nonnecessity.

A More Perfect Disunion

It may come as a surprise, though, that I now want to say that in my reading there is no immediate reason to jettison Marx's divide between necessary material production and free activity after this material production has been accomplished. *I instead seek a way to make such a divide more meaningful and desirable.* This is so in three ways.

First, there is Marx's original positing of the realm of necessity to be divided (somehow) from the realm of nonnecessity, a discerning of time spent on what it is necessary to spend time on from time that can be devoted to free play and human development for itself. Why is the discernment good to think? The critique of the Gotha socialists is instructive. The politics of exploitation is a powerful incentive to posit the immediate possession of the fruits of labor. But Marx recognizes the potential for felt need, for consumption, to overexpand, to spill over into a self-centered sense of deserving. He asks, therefore, that the production of our essential being be nonidentical with consumption—a politics of restraint. How is this different from the self-imposed restraint of the miser? For Marx the social has an ontological reality on par with the individual's. Individuals are seen not just as producing themselves but rather as producing the society as such. Each thus is productive of more than herself or himself. When Marx therefore calls for a distinct quality of necessary production, we ought to think of this society as such as what he's got in mind. This is, though, a political heuristic because the society of associated production would not rest on this minimum. Marx has no concept of the necessary in and of itself, as if this subsisted in a known basket of needs and in contradistinction to the fictitious needs of capital. It is a relative idea. In this way of giving meaning to the quandary of the divide between freedom and necessity, the solution is as surprising as is the unintended problem that Marx produces in the first place: freedom in the sphere of necessity is, as André Gorz suggests, the freedom to choose restraint.[13] What is one restraining one's self from? From the potential to live in isolation from society's essential being of mutual dependence. From an isolation that can only ever be feigned. That is the lesson of the miser. He would isolate himself amid the very social relationships he in fact depends upon. But his actions carry a truth to a certain extent: the necessary nonidentity between production and consumption. The society of associated producers would be tasked with turning this figure of the miser right side up.

Second, there also is, by virtue of cooperative labor, a principle I do not see Marx abandoning in his notion of associated production: that a realm of nonnecessity (surprise, serendipity, etc.) also exists within the realm of necessity. *Nonnecessity thus exists on both sides of the line that ostensibly divides freedom from necessity.* This is essentially different from the recursive way in which pleasures experienced after material production is over would create new needs for the realm of necessity to produce (i.e., different from arguing that enjoyment of music would spur production of the instruments with which to make music). The both-sidedness of nonnecessity lessens the problem of rendering labor abject all over again while allowing Marx his point that it is wise (pragmatic) for a society based upon associated production to not presume its capacity to reproduce itself. We allow him to posit such a society as self-critical on this point as a way of keeping the *problem* of value alive, as opposed to considering it solved.

Third is the idea that freedom, in Marx's first sense (here presumed and which by rights should maybe count as the very first of these specifications), will eventually discover that what grounds it is also what limits it.[14] Marx suggests that in the society of associated production, the growth of needs will be kept up with by the growth of productive forces. In this sense, the realm of true freedom can always keep its grounding in material production, an essential condition of possibility. Note, though, that Marx already posits a distance between these spheres, not an identity: as seen in chapter 3's discussion of the trinity formula, productive forces will "keep pace with the development of needs." But there is every reason to think that these productive forces play an even more active role, including an inhibiting one. For what Marx must also be saying is that what freedom desires must be kept in check by existing productive forces. In other words, freedom is only as good as the productive forces that can be developed to meet it. If this is not so, then Marx is just another idealist: all your dreams will come true! But it *is* possible to imagine manifestations of freedom that we will never have. It would be good to productively deal with the limits of the possible. (Here, I take limit to be a symptom of life. It is not an absolute known beforehand, not imposed from the outside, but is discovered in the acts and forms of living.) It seems to me such an idea lurks at the edges of the value idea and has always been a part of what value is about. This means that freedom—this notion of human development for itself—ought to be better than what Marx himself proposes. In any event, the two realms of necessity and freedom are not perfectly tuned to each other but are defined necessarily by the distance between them and a politics to potentially bridge them.[15] This distance maintains each as a semiautonomous realm, each of which never fully speaks for the other. Value must involve the job of discovering this distance.

Conclusion

At this point, a new crux for the matter of value appears: that a crucial role of the value concept, its nonutopian function, is our use of it to discover the limit point of social formations—that is, the discovery of the terms (in the enabling and constraining sense) under which the social is or can be lived. Consider the country that has been crossed. Capitalism breaks up old ties and allegiances and creates a new set of social relations to be lived out in a new way, new with respect to newly imposed limits but also new openings for further development. This is seen time and again in chapter 3, which is built around *Capital*, volume 3, and in the various textual sites touched upon in this chapter. Marx sometimes approaches the matter with surprising equanimity, too, conceding that people cannot live out their sociality until they have created it—thus, capital's historical function to create new conditions for sociality. Of course, social bonds cannot possibly be really lived (i.e., their potential to be other than what they are is not seized upon) until capitalism is abolished and associated production takes its place. Yet Marx says enough during these calculations, especially where the qualities of necessity and freedom upon which the desired future hangs are concerned, that the basis upon which these truly social relations can really be lived would also inevitably have to be rediscovered as a point at which the social (as a ceaseless becoming) cannot be lived, a limit point where the social ceases to be represented. And this it seems to me is a new trap Marx lays for himself in setting out a certain vision of associated production. In what sense can this kind of production ever solve the conundrum of value? If it cannot do so definitively—for the reconstructions of necessity and freedom I attempt here are still too much of a virtuous circle—then there seems to be only one choice in moving forward without illusions: to value this limit point itself.

Part III

5

The Value Hypothesis

Three Scenes for a Political Imaginary of Value

In the summer of 1868, Marx wrote a letter to his then-friend Ludwig Kugelmann that gathers together many of the core themes I try to ferret out in this book. In frank annoyance with his detractors, he writes:

> All that palaver about the necessity of proving the con-
> cept of value comes from complete ignorance both of
> the subject dealt with and of scientific method. Every
> child knows that a nation which ceased to work, I will
> not say for a year, but even for a few weeks, would per-
> ish. Every child knows, too, that the masses of products
> corresponding to the different needs require different
> and quantitatively determined masses of the total labor
> of society. That this necessity of the distribution of social
> labor in definite proportions cannot possibly be done
> away with by a particular form of social production but
> can only change the mode of its appearance, is self-
> evident. . . . The history of the theory certainly shows
> that the concept of the value relation has always been
> the same—more or less clear, hedged more or less with
> illusions or scientifically more or less definite. . . . The
> essence of bourgeois society consists precisely in this,
> that *a priori* there is no conscious social regulation of
> production. The rational and naturally necessary asserts
> itself only as a blindly working average. And then the

vulgar economist thinks he has made a great discovery when, as against the revelation of the inner interconnection, he proudly claims that in appearance things look different. In fact, he boasts that he holds fast to appearance, and takes it for the ultimate. Why, then, have any science at all?

But the matter has also another background. Once the interconnection is grasped, all theoretical belief in the permanent necessity of existing conditions collapses before their collapse in practice.[1]

Marx places the important tenets in Kugelmann's hand. Value and capital do not exhaust each other and are not coterminous. Value, while appearing differently in different modes of production (including the ironic failure to appear and yet have itself rescued by natural necessity), is a domain of thought and critique applicable to no single sort of mode of production. Instead, it is a problem for them all, an enduring problem that—even though Marx describes it from within the moment of capitalism—any society must come to grips with. And yet societies are not restricted to producing only one idea of what value is and may not have an idea of it as such. Marx's encounters with bourgeois political economy, with utopian socialist political economy, and indeed with Kugelmann exemplify this. And though Marx makes a plea for science, he affirms that this is itself a terrain of struggle. The "concept of the value relation," as Marx puts it, is conceived by him against the background of his own times and that of "another background"—of the future, of associated production. All of this is consistent with the archive of multivalent statements whose reading I have tried to assemble here.

At the same time, this reading indicates that it would be best to approach Marx's letter critically, seeing it not just as a defense of value but as a statement about the problem of value—namely, that it is one thing to grasp a necessary and self-evident interconnection between the distribution of social labor and masses of products but quite another to make the interconnection appear properly. For good reason Marx avers on the matter, since it is a question not simply of planning but of opportunities and outcomes that arise amid struggles that will have considerable say in producing the different needs to which Marx alludes.[2] That is why in *The German Ideology*, penned in the 1840s and today a beacon for those Marx-inspired writers, such as Hardt and Negri, who have rallied around notions of the common, Marx and Engels write that "communism is for us not a *state of affairs* which is to be established, an *ideal* to which reality will have to adjust itself. We call communism the *real* movement which abolishes the present state of things. The conditions of this movement result from the premises now in existence."[3] Just the same though, Marx says enough about what he means by associated labor that in so doing he shows how the concept of the value relation must be a matter of lasting concern—and not always in a manner he intends. His handling of the issues concerning how freedom and necessity relate to and transform each other and his raising the matter of the mutually conditioning relationship between social desires and forces of production—these concerns elicited in the previous chapter—indicate that the trick is less to overrule the rule of value or to solve the value problem than to keep the problem of value alive by inscribing the notion of a limit into any conceivable such solution. In the terms of Marx's letter to Kugelmann, the issue becomes how a collapse of "belief in the permanent necessity of existing conditions," including those conditions existing in whatever comes after capitalism, might arise from the concept of the value relation itself, thereby inscribing into this concept the notion of its permanent necessity.

Working value up into such a political imaginary is a tall order, pursuable from different directions and with different intent. I pursue just one, the possibility that value, *in explicitly involving a limit point*, would be desirable because it could be pleasurable. Marx implies that this limit point, the threshold in which the nonnecessity of existing conditions becomes apparent, is comprised of a sequence: collapse of belief occurs before collapse in practice. I will not hold myself to such a constraint. Belief and practice might be too tangled up in each other for such a determination to hold. Moreover, as I hope to show, the entanglement is one not only of belief and practice but also of the social relation between people and *things*, the certainty of which is surely less clear than Marx's tetchy letter lets on.

Over and against the broad relevance of value that I propose here is the suggestion by some writers that value is to be overthrown in favor of some more genuine production that is beyond measure. This position, which has become popular as both a way of reading Marx and as a political position in influential books by Negri (*Marx beyond Marx*) and by Hardt and Negri (*Multitude* and, perhaps, *Commonwealth*), is not one that I am ready to adopt. The mode of value-theoretic thought saturates Marx's writing such that I do not think the notion of measure ever is really forsaken by him and, however vexed, with good justification. In fairness, talk of value has not completely disappeared. *Commonwealth* in fact speaks of the need for an alternative theory of value.

> [Such a value] is created when resistance becomes overflowing, creative, and boundless and thus when human activity exceeds and determines a rupture in the balance of power. Value is created, consequently, when the relations between the constituent elements of the biopolitical process and structure of biopower are thrown out of balance. When control over development, which the state and the collective organisms of capital assume to define their own legitimacy, is no longer able to hold back the resistance of the multitude, labor-power, and the whole set of social singularities, only then will there be value.[4]

Rendering *value* as synonymous with *boundless, overflowing*, and *creative* activity (although this meaning is not clear) does not easily sit with the attempt to come to grips with value as a procedure for the discovery of social limit points. But what these approaches, one with its emphasis on overcoming and the other with its stress on an interest in being overcome, might have in common is an emphasis on pleasure—that is, a move away from value as unwelcomed discipline. Furthermore, if my gambit has merit, it could also be likely that any society will encounter its limit in the very form of relationality it assumes. What then? Might a positive valence for such a limit be a way forward?

I hope the chapters heretofore are useful in showing some of the variety through which Marx registers the generic concern, now so evident in the letter to Kugelmann, for "the concept of the value relation." The warrant for the question of why it could be desirable to construct a notion of value that actually esteems the limits of social formations might also now be salient. In what remains I would like to give these purposes a determinate shape by reconstructing a few of what I call the scenes of value in Marx. These scenes recapitulate some of the variety of Marx's value-theoretic formulations, but they do so in such a way as to illuminate a recurring obsession Marx has: What does it mean that social relations and social labor, including their effect of producing society as such and society's potential to become otherwise, can become thinglike? The role played by thinglike power in Marx's ideas about value must now be emphasized more than before. Not only does its recurrence draw attention to the possibility for radicalizing thinglike power by approaching it as a locus of pleasurable experience. Marx's interest in, so to say, object lessons renders value-theoretic some of the most interesting assertions he makes about his world and, by extension, ours. But what do I mean by "scenes"? Just as Marx loved a good aphorism or an evocative turn of phrase—there is a short section of the *Grundrisse* exclusively devoted to a list of aphorisms, and as Fredric Jameson stresses, one does not read in Marx for long before the wordsmith appears[5]—Marx also was a scenic thinker. Certain of these scenes are famous and rather dramatic, as at the end of chapter 6 of volume 1 of *Capital*, where Marx has us follow the wage earner and a certain Mr. Moneybags as they depart the "noisy sphere" of the market and enter the "hidden abode of production" behind the factory gates.[6] The point of course is to demonstrate how C . . . M . . . C will mutate into M . . . C . . . M'. The scene reminds us that process and objective form are essential here. The exchange of values requires a form—money—and money requires, if it is to be augmented through market exchange, a certain form of production: that predicated on wage labor as the dominant form of remunerable labor. Production requires the form of an agent provocateur, Mr. Moneybags, and an actual producer to accompany him, the possessor of labor power. Marx has moved from an abstraction to a ground where he imagines (on the reader's behalf) this abstraction working itself out. Most of Marx's set pieces are neither famous nor dramatic, but these object lessons are nonetheless good to think with. But the following scenes are, in fact, object lessons of an especially figurative kind, involving Marx's interest in the choreography of objects in the everyday life of different sorts of social relations. These scenes are places where Marx's politics are expressed as an invitation to feel and think our way through a very particular, grounded situation where not only belief and practice (to take some language from the Kugelmann letter) but also *thing* convene. An interesting point about these scenes is that they show belief, practice, and thing as not lining up. This incommensurability is what makes them scenes, and what is especially noteworthy about them from my standpoint is the way the objects in them get cut off from what they are supposed to be doing, from what they ostensibly represent by way of belief and practice. Objects seem ready to move, to break out, to be charged with potential energy. In moving through the scenes in the following three sections, my objective is to highlight Marx as keenly interested in object lessons of this sort, both of the kind that shows how capitalist value works (or not) and of the kind that if read a certain way, points toward a potential beyond capitalism and, as counterintuitive as this must sound so far, toward the politics and ultimately the potential pleasures of the inevitable shortfalls and limits of social becoming.

The Office of the Fabulously Wealthy Banker Herr v. Rothschild

The *Grundrisse* offers only the most fleeting of views, but the scene is pointed. Marx takes a literal peek into Rothschild's office and discovers the contradiction between money as representative of wealth for its possessor and as representative of value for purposes of commodity circulation, hanging on Rothschild's very wall.

> To the degree that money develops in its various roles, i.e. that wealth as such becomes the general measure of the worth of individuals, there develops the drive to display it, hence the display of gold and silver as representatives of wealth; in the same way Herr v. Rothschild displays as his proper emblem, I think, two banknotes of 100,000 each, mounted in a frame. The barbarian display of gold etc. is only a more naïve form of this modern one, since it takes place with less regard to gold as money. Here still the simple *glitter*. There a premeditated point. The point being that it is *not* used as money; here the form antithetical to circulation is what is important.[7]

Even after capitalist society has transcended the valuation of gold on the basis of its materiality, by now valuing it instead in its money form, this society cannot escape the worship of materiality as such. The dullness of paper notes still retains the old "simple *glitter.*" The capitalist, Marx concludes, requires a primitive, barbaric form of value, but it comes with a cost. The notes cannot have their glitter—that is, cannot serve the function of the display of wealth—unless they are withdrawn from circulation and cease to be real money. True barbarian display does not contain such a contradiction; display there (then) takes place "with less regard to gold as money." But now it is precisely the money function that is denied, and the glitter form that is reinstated. The scenario echoes what many commentators on the *Grundrisse* have said about that work, that Marx's concept of capitalism perceives the survival and reworking of older social forms, upon which capital is parasitic for its own purposes. More than this, such parasitism is costly for capital, "interrupting" its logic, in Vinay Gidwani's apt expression.[8] Thus, in this scene the tendency toward the display of wealth continues in capitalism in a disruptive way. Money has reached a point and, no less, come to an actual place where it ceases to represent the social forces and processes that it ostensibly embodies. It requires the contradiction that it stand still and become a *thing* again. This thing, Rothschild's bank note, has in sum a very special quality in Marx's eyes. In needing to move and stand still at the same time, it shows itself as deprived of essence, lacking self-identity. It is at war with itself and shot through with contradiction. It will never have self-evident existence.

But this also is only a conventional scene, a view onto value as a concept of the limit to which social power can gain adequate representation in capitalism, a rehearsal of what has already been said and shown: we know the writing is on the wall before reading it in Rothschild's office. In Marx making a note of Rothschild's display, however, *he is himself displaying that display*—showing his interest in the things of this world. With what is Marx complicit that he notices what is hanging on Rothschild's wall? If we care to notice, Marx has established the beginning of a chain, invoked a series of possible affections. Furthermore, if the meaning of the framed money is that it is the survival and reworking of an old form, a contradictory form lacking self-evidence, no less, what older forms is Marx himself in the business of reworking? Past discussion (the time-chit) shows that indeed money is exactly one of those forms. So now also comes the question, *What role do objects and their display have in Marx's thought, and what contradictory elements might they bring along with them when he seems to like the display he sees?* The next scenario ups the ante on these matters.

The Hall Where French Communist Workers Gather after Work

> When communist workmen associate with each other, propaganda, etc., is the first end. But at the same time, as a result of this association, they acquire a new need—the need for society—and what appears as a means becomes an end. You can observe this practical process in its most splendid results whenever you see French socialist workers together. Such things as smoking, drinking,

eating, etc., are no longer mere means of contact or
means that bring them together. Company, association,
and conversation, which again has society as its end,
are enough for them; the brotherhood of man is no mere
phrase with them, but a fact of life, and the nobility of
man shines upon us from their work hardened bodies.[9]

Marx inserts this passage in a section of *The Economic and
Philosophic Manuscripts of 1844* devoted to the "meaning of
human requirements." The section is a critique of needs in the
commodity society and the way that working-class opposition
is formed in response to an ideology that says needs are being filled, or can be filled, through commodity production. First,
Marx makes the point that capitalism has stunted our notion of
what real need even is: the real need is to develop our species
being, to never accept its present form as its final form, and
in fact to deny finality of form to species being. Such a development would rightly involve the stimulation of all our senses
through worldly engagement, a refinement of hearing, taste,
touch, smell, sight, speech, and so on such that a person (the
social individual) becomes more and more well-rounded. Marx
describes this in the manuscripts as a process whereby man
becomes more "universal" the more he interacts with nature
"universally." This is, he argues, what real need is all about—a
heightening of the human senses, an increase of relationality
among them, among human beings whose senses are so height-
ened and interrelated, and among these human beings and nonhuman nature—in short, a broadening of the conditions of possibility, conditions of which human beings are, at the end of the
day (and before the next day begins), an effect.[10] The manuscripts contrast these real needs with the meager requirements
of workers to reproduce their capacity to work in the capitalist factory, where the machine has "adapted itself to the weak-
ness of the human being" (95). Bourgeois society and political
economists, in particular, not only accept this restricted sense
of need but have developed positive ideological formulations of
it that have led us to believe that restriction *is* fulfillment. This
whole process is what Marx calls estrangement, and to fight

against it, one goes through it in accordance with specific premises in existence. "Naturally the transcendence of estrangement always proceeds from that form of the estrangement which is the dominant power: in Germany, self consciousness; in France, equality, because politics . . ." and so on (99). Further, Marx notes, estrangement cannot be transcended only in consciousness, as this would only entrench estrangement all the more "the more one is conscious of it as such" (99). (Thus, to circle back to a point made much earlier in chapter 1, mere critique of the commodity fetish would in this new sense be an estranging act.) It must be abolished in practice and replaced by something actually positive, a new foundation for human being. What Marx is searching for and believes he has found are examples of the immediate producers developing a consciousness of the dominant form of estrangement in their society and a practice that takes them beyond that consciousness to the discovery of an alternative mode of existence. This is the importance of French socialists discovering, in the act of gathering together, a form of brotherhood and society surpassing the capitalist state form of *liberté, égalité, fraternité* that Marx alludes to. They not only discover this trio as a real need but, transcending mere phrase, apparently live it in their gathering together as such.

Interestingly, though, in the last sentence describing the scene, Marx sets himself the task of representing this process to his readers, as if wanting to tell them what it all means. For the purpose he chooses an uncanny metaphor, one that smacks of the money form of value: "the nobility of man shines upon us from their work-hardened bodies," as if these bodies are metal-like and that this very form represents to us (i.e., is the currency of) the sociality of labor that they really have become. (This is a precursor to Marx's argument in the chapter on money in the *Grundrisse.*) At the same time, there is a universalizing urge in Marx's description: it is *Frenchmen* who gather but the nobility of *man* that reflects off of them. It is a fitting image for Marx to use when the point is that struggles shaped by local circumstances will need to branch out in some manner if they are to remain viable, let alone posit some new foundation. More than this even, the suggestion is that in the very practice of gathering and in sensing something new in the raw need for this, real human being per se emerges. But in allowing the image of value (money) to structure the scene, the disjunction between the forward trajectory Marx sees in this workers' gathering and the frozen, work-hardened form that would represent the trajectory is glaringly obvious.

Some questions are, then, as follows: What is it that accounts for the nobility of man in the scene anyway? It appears to be that brotherhood, etc., have achieved actual fact and have surpassed being a mere phrase (of the French state, in this case), but if this is so, then how do these bodies, hardened by work in capitalism, fit? What is their role, and why does Marx mention them at all? What I want to get at are the limits of representing in a value-laden image the direct producers of commodities caught in the act of associating. What is gained, and what does it cost to pose association in a trope of value of this kind? For if Marx's drift is that the production of bodies in capitalism is based on stunted needs, how can the bodies that result convey the nobility of man? It would seem to be just the opposite; they convey man in an ignoble state. Nor does it work to say that these bodies are made noble by their suffering, since that is precisely a bourgeois perspective. If we say, conversely, that the nobility of man, as in man's freedom, necessarily rests upon a base of hard work, well, we have already seen in chapter 4 the trap set by that line of thought—namely, work is rendered abject against the greater freedom to be found after material needs are met. I previously suggest that we can free ourselves from that trap only by peering into the realm of production where the experience of freedom (nonnecessity) might also emerge in equally valued measure. But unfortunately, the scene Marx offers here is after work. It could be that what Marx means is that the workers' hardened bodies are like the battle-scarred bodies of noble fighters; the wound becomes a badge of honor. Their nobility results from what they have given up in order to come as far as they have, on their own behalf and the behalf of all the oppressed. If so, this places the scene dangerously close to the politics of exploitation, in which exploitation directly translates into notions of deservingness. And indeed, there is something cloistered and club-like about the setting. There is no indication of precisely how to get from the fraternity of the workers' hall (or café or meeting room or what have you) to that of all humankind. More problematically, though, Marx analyzes the labor process in capitalism as weakening, not hardening, the human being. One senses a clash of aphorism, an unconvincing phrase, a confusion concerning what work these bodies actually do as a signification of Marx's politics and political economy. What exactly is the *object* lesson?

The question answers itself. By this I mean the difference between whatever new framework these French socialist workers are said to have discovered and the one Marx employs to communicate its meaning is a highly charged difference. It is as if there are two voices speaking in the scene, the voice of the workers and that of Marx. And there is a rupture between these voices that itself needs to be paid attention to. To be precise, it seems to me that through these voicings Marx is staging two different tropes of value. One is the trope, close perhaps to Hardt and Negri's, that inquires into how value works after hours, a trope of value that sees value as emerging, unmediated, in experience itself, directly lived rather than given over to an alien entity.[11] Furthermore, it is value reworked into a newly overdetermined society of associated producers where it does not need to represent itself to itself. With this a new meaning is given to the idea that value does not stalk about with a label on its head. This is what Marx infamously writes in the first volume of *Capital* about the hieroglyphic of value in the commodity society, that value can manifest itself only through indirection, chaos, and crisis. And yet now that value emerges as directly lived in associated production, it still need not stalk about with a label. This presumption nonetheless is problematic and would remain troublingly so were it not that another value trope (or Marx's second voice) was on the scene: Marx's manifest need, probably a Hegelian one, to represent and to see as a *thing*—as objectified form—the social powers that have been put to work and to see this as better than capitalism.[12] In Marx's rendering of the very bodies of these workers as glittering things is there not his own Rothschild-like display of money-of-a-kind, the perpetuation of fetish? Voiced in the one idiom of "money," he offers a critique of capital and a statement of its being surpassed in one and the same image. But the rupture between Marx raising, per se, the subject of these communist workers together and his representation of their fixity signals that he never quite works out, let alone dispels, the tension between designating associated production as a moment of pure becoming and seeing the necessity to keep accounts of the determinants of value in associated production. These are different sides of value that Marx cannot let go of. But should he have? Is there no way to simply say that this tension just *is* and that it *shall be*? That it expresses the diverse modalities through which he explores the concept of the value relation? And that it expresses not only Marx's keen interest in the imminent pleasures of communist politics and moments to be seized (those French communist workmen) but also a just as keen interest in the critique of pleasures should they prove undercutting (recall his critique of the Gotha socialists)? An essential thing is, it seems, that the two moments of pure becoming and keeping accounts ought always to be present and kept from disappearing into each other. This implies, however, the presence of a third voice that might be capable of maintaining a rupture between those other two voices, a critical attitude or practice that minds the gap and keeps value tropes apart for strategic purposes.

I add a word of caution, though. Perhaps, it is only that Marx is playing around with the idea of the fetish, trying to develop an alternative meaning for it. Indeed, a few paragraphs earlier than the one in question, in a passage that lends itself to our reading the shine of the work-hardened body in the idiom of money in the first place, Marx notes that the "nations which are still dazzled by the sensuous splendor of precious metals and are therefore still fetish-worshipers of metal money, are not yet fully developed money-nations" (98). What they do not yet see is that it is not the physical form of money that gives it its value; rather, per volume 1 of *Capital*, money is a form of value because value is already presumed in it. As we know, value rests on social labor that the commodity, including money, merely embodies or tries to embody. What Marx seems to suggest is that if one wants a fetish, these French socialist workers' bodies, at rest no less, make a *better* one. For all of this, the scene still is highly fraught and indeterminate. Like metallic money, body money, so to speak, also fails to represent the march of social power and falls outside it as a displayed thing—it is ripped out of the very process of production whereby relationality increases and where real need has its immanent becoming. Thus, if these workmen are socialist/communist because they work at a cooperative factory of some kind or at a capitalist factory but have joined a socialist/communist league (Marx does not say which), Marx repeats the problem that real freedom is found after work is done. There is also the curious statement that "company, conversation, and association" are sufficient for them, an oddly dematerialized depiction of need and effacement of sensuous, material needs production. In short, the scene has Marx's politics written all over it but is riddled with gaps. It is a signification that fails to signify, in which phrase and content are curiously cut off from each other, although the signification does animate all over again some of the crucial problems that value faces.

The general conundrum, even when reading the scene on its face—a group of workers hanging out after work, having some drinks and a smoke, plotting political maneuvers and sensing this as a need fulfillment in itself—is that a past form (the work-hardened body) mediates the process whereby these new desires and needs are identified and lived out in the way that they are, and Marx says nothing of substance here about that. Or rather, what he says is of or about substance but remains insubstantial. He implies a connection between this form and the social relations it is enmeshed in without explaining what that connection really is. The scene is supposed to speak the connection, perhaps. But really, it is an image that takes over and is the putative substance of the politics. This is an unsustainable moment. (As Althusser warns in *Reading "Capital,"* it is precisely relationships that are so very difficult to see, and that is why they require concepts.) Instead notice, then, that if social power is represented in these bodies but social power is a moving, changing phenomenon, then its form requires transformation. It is in the very nature of the social to require this. And if transformation itself requires a form, then there can never be an end to the need for transformation. Could there ever be an end to this tension?[13] Won't bodies (i.e., living labor that acts and is acted upon in labor and that results in a certain fixity of bodies and things) always discover they have been formed in this way and not another and that the very sociality that frees individuals from their fetters as private individuals, as Marx puts it, is implicated? (The same point applies to Deleuze and Guattari's notion of the socius or the full body. These terms describe the fetters that necessarily, though not absolutely, inhibit social becoming.)[14]

Now, the question of why the problem of these gaps and elisions cannot be resolved could be answered by reminding ourselves that in that *other* image of cooperative labor encountered in volume 1 of *Capital*, in which the "spirits" are "animated" and bodies always are recombining, Marx has solved with *that* imaginary the problem that has emerged here. But surely this only displaces the question of fixity to another scale. And the temptation to consider the matter of keeping accounts of pure becoming solved in this way should be resisted. There are, as I argue, two voices and a rupture between them that needs to be thought through (and, no less, perpetuated). But before leaving the noisy, smoky sphere of our communist workmen, it is necessary to be as clear as possible about what I have been conjecturing. This is, minus some of the finer points, that in this sphere Marx first speaks value in the trope of the real experience of becoming—real because life activity no longer is alien. So to say, I, if a communist workman, am resolved to this activity and to my brethren, and it and they are resolved to me. But in a second and, indeed, in a nanosecond-later voicing of value, Marx occludes real activity that would be sufficient to itself by taking its measure in the form of the work-hardened body. Marx disbelieves the sufficient-to-itself and would also want an index with which to *know*. Finally, the rupture between these voicings is caused by Marx being unable to conceptualize (*in this scene*) the role of object, form, and objectification in convincingly desirable terms. Why see activity in fixed terms, as a fixture? What does calling attention to objectification here add that would not result in something else (real activity) being taken away? *What does the index do that Marx wants to know?* In essence, if objectification is to be really put to work—and this is what Marx very much wants—it is put to the wrong kind of work in this scene. Yet Marx is an alluring enough thinker to keep his readers engaged in all three of these wagers because of the way they mutually shock and poke at each other—that is to say, they are each other's questions. But to put this in a still more provocative and convincing light, I suggest going to another scene, singular, I think, in Marx's writings.

The Scene of Greek Art

I will enter as carefully as possible and, at first, obliquely. The text now is the *Grundrisse*. For the Marx of the *Grundrisse*, a mode of production is typified by the way in which social forms and processes existing in a prior period—or simply in a different, adjacent society, whether prior or contemporary—are reworked into a new complex formation. As Marx works this idea out things become very strange indeed. A mode of production is, Marx insists, never a static state but a dynamic and contradictory interrelation of social practices. It is characteristic of this dynamism that processes which may have had prominence in an earlier social formation might lose that prominence later. Or processes of little consequence before may achieve greater moment in the future. This is what Marx means when he writes that the same category can occupy "divergent positions . . . in different social stages," an idea to which Althusser, borrowing from Freud, famously gave the name "overdetermination."[15] As categories (discreet social processes) are reworked Marx stresses they are also no longer quite the same. Money—what it is and what is done with it—is a classic example, of course. Its display by a capitalist is a sort of survival from and reinvention of past practice; its embodiment/dissolution by associated labor is its ostensible future. The whole process is riddled with indeterminacy, though, as there is no saying what will become of a particular social practice and how it will be reworked. This makes the capitalist mode of production what Gidwani calls an "anxious whole." Capitalism is never fully itself but rather out of joint with itself. It is shot through with logics not of its own making; capital must call upon these in predatory fashion in order to establish its circulation.[16] In somewhat similar fashion, Louis Althusser and Étienne Balibar reread *Capital*. That is, capitalism's organizing force is not unilateral but can work only as a constellation of forces and practices that constitute and articulate to each other. Famously, the economic is determinate in the "last instance" of the making of capitalist social formations, but infamously, the last moment "never comes."[17] Time stalls; the force that seems to give society its temporality is denied, at the end of the day, that opportunity. As a result, the future seems to be more open and rich with possibility. Indeed, time is turned upside down and inside out, for Marx's notion of history is not only stridently nonteleological but curiously flattened. Consider his memorable idea in the introduction to the *Grundrisse* that the future is the key to the past rather than the other way around—that is, only the unfolding of events makes clear what the past is as a force in the world.[18] This means that the present (or future) reworking of the social forms and practices of prior periods is part and parcel of how they worked in the first place. Namely, they worked as potentials—that is, as processes that *could be* reworked. Again, the future is key to the past. Fine! But no sooner does Marx lay out this general conception than he discovers an intriguing, perhaps even nagging, specification of it—the possibility of practices that cannot seem to be pegged to their own time . . . or any other. I want to suggest in what follows that these practices, worked into an expressed desideratum, might serve to construct that third voice summoned up at the end of the scene concerning those communist workmen. This voice, this desideratum, is an integral and, for my purposes, culminating part of Marx's value repertoire.

Contemplating the overdetermined relation of art to the other social practices dominant at the time of art's creation, Marx writes in the *Grundrisse*, "As regards art, it is well-known that some of its peaks by no means correspond to the general development of society; nor do they therefore to the material substructure, the skeleton as it were of its organization" (149). Moreover, such peaks are "only possible at an early stage of development [of society]." Certain developments are, in other words, out of synch. And if they are peaks, then there are questions as to their continuing status. Where is an artistic peak to go, especially if one has a progressive outlook on it and wants it to go, progressively, somewhere? Or shall it be consigned to the status of irrelevant antiquity with no particular purchase on us now? After all, Marx is no dispassionate observer. It is one thing to argue for the withering away of the state but quite another to argue for beautiful art objects and our regard for them to vanish into thin air. "The difficulty," Marx states, "lies only in the general formulation of these contradictions. As soon as they are reduced to specific questions they are already explained" (150).

The stage is now set for the third scene, Marx's meditation on such a specific question, ancient Greek art, that immediately follows this passage from the *Grundrisse*. (This is not so much a scene as contemplation of a class of object against its background. But maybe we can think of Marx in the British Museum, wandering away from its reading room, where he filled his notebooks, to look at the famed Elgin Marbles or other examples of Greek art. Or if we prefer, we might recall Marx as a student in Berlin, whose classically themed architecture—courtesy of the Enlightenment influence of Frederick the Great—Marx preferred over the Gothic revivals of the day.[19]) First, as if to qualify his statement that artistic peaks have no correspondence to their less-developed contexts, Marx observes that Greek art, whose inspiration was Greek mythology, would not be possible in the modern age of industrial production, with its quite different conception of natural forces. "Is the conception of nature and of social relations which underlies Greek imagination and therefore Greek art possible where there are self-acting mules, railways, locomotives and electric telegraphs? What is a Vulcan compared with Roberts and Co., Jupiter compared with the lightning conductor, and Hermes compared with Crédit mobilier?" (150). But before definitively resolving the problem of the disjuncture between what he insists is the undeveloped state of Greek society generally and the highly developed form of its art, which seems to defy its mythological habitus (I return to this point later), Marx simply and very quickly moves on to suggest that the more interesting problem is actually "not that of understanding how Greek art and epic poetry are associated with certain forms of social development." Instead, *"the difficulty is that they still give us aesthetic pleasure and are in certain respects regarded as a standard and an unattainable ideal"* (150; emphasis added).

It is a mystery, then, what to do about art produced in this, a peak period of its development. How are we to think its relevance? How are we to appropriate it, develop it, work it into some new complex of articulations? How should future peoples do such things? Or to phrase the question in terms fitting the *Grundrisse*, how should the future *survive* Greek art? How, precisely when Marx stipulates that Greek art is simultaneously a measure and unattainable? The risk of emulation here is quite plain.

> An adult can not become a child again, or he becomes childish. But does the naiveté of the child not give him pleasure, and does not he himself endeavor to reproduce the child's veracity on a higher level? Does not in every epoch the child represent the character of the period in its natural veracity? Why should not the historical childhood of humanity, where it attained its most beautiful form, exert an eternal charm because it is a stage that will never recur? The charm [Greek] art has for us does not conflict with the immature stage of the society in which it originated. On the contrary its charm is a consequence of this and is inseparably linked with the fact that the immature social conditions which gave rise, and which alone could give rise, to this art cannot recur. (151)

In my reading, these are some of the most interesting passages in Marx's texts. Before plunging in, though, the seriousness of the phenomenon Marx is treating is worth establishing. That there is something potentially serious at stake in "childishly" resurrecting aesthetic forms is, as Terry Eagleton points out in his own reflections on these passages, a prominent aspect of the essay Marx had written only a few years before beginning the *Grundrisse* (i.e., *The Eighteenth Brumaire of Louis Bonaparte*, an all-out attack on the political, social, and *aesthetic* manifestations of empire in the France of Napoleon III).[20] These manifestations, Marx writes, "weighed like a nightmare on the brains of the living," as Louis-Napoléon Bonaparte attempted to legitimate his despotic rule through infantile and farcical resurrection of historico-artistic code—among other means.[21] The stakes are also exposed in the thematic continuity between Marx's meditation on the uses (or not) of Greek art, placed at the very end of the introduction to the *Grundrisse*, and the topic that immediately follows in "The Chapter on Money"—namely, the critique of the childish labor money schemes of the socialist utopians. (Marx also penned his notes on Greek art and labor money only a couple of months apart from each other.) The obvious shared theme is that the circulation of important social objects in time and space has lessons to teach: if we are going to give them power, we should at least go into our relationship with them in full cognizance of their social substance.

And yet a further point prompts close attention to the scene of Greek art: Marx is writing about an activity that is a crucial aspect of production in what he dubs "the realm of freedom," the sphere where surplus activity is rewritten as utterly necessary for species being to manifest itself. That this concern touches ground in the connection between Marx's musings on Greek art and his own biography is worth briefly noticing. Marx took aesthetics seriously throughout his life. His notes on Greek art in the *Grundrisse* reflect the differences he felt early on with the prominent German critic Friedrich Schiller on this very same subject. Some of Schiller's very phrases (and Hegel's for that matter) were reworked by Marx in those notes, as Margaret Rose demonstrates in her meticulous and fascinating reconstruction of Marx's "lost aesthetic."[22] As a young man in Prussia, Marx was caught up in a struggle between Nazarene and Hellene aesthetic formations. The Nazarene tradition, traceable (in varied ways) not only to Schiller but to Kant, to Marx's professors at university, and to the Prussian monarchy of the

Friedrich Wilhelms III and IV, who lent their material support
to it, essentially was a revival of Christian spiritualism in art, a
preference to see the mind and spirit liberated from the body,
from matter as such. Against the Nazarene principle, Heinrich
Heine (who had coined the term) pitted the Hellene. Heine, a
writer-critic and follower of Saint-Simon, scandalized the Nazarene establishment with his preference for Hellenistic sensual-
istic qualities in art, such as those manifest in Delacroix's 1831
painting *Liberty Guiding the People*, whose central female figure expresses in her very *flesh* the "wild energy of the people . . .
throwing off a heavy burden."[23] So thought Heine, with Marx
very much in agreement. Marx greatly admired Heine's writings;
they influenced his own. For Heine and Marx—and, really, who
can blame them?—it was flesh that needed liberation from spirit
(the inversion is by now well known).

Therefore, contrary to art being merely art, to art being a curiosity and Greek art being an especially puzzling curiosity, we
are compelled to think it as essential, as a sine qua non relation
of the life worth living. Artistic production is a feature of the
world to be won, and Greek art is (for Marx and many other
members of his educated class, though not all, as we have just
seen) a peak of artistic production *and* a stake in the political
struggle over cultural production. Has Marx any choice but to
think it? And for French communist workmen who might pick
up on this thread, what does the "charm" of Greek art hold out
for them? For that must also be Marx's question. And as for us,
what is revealed by Marx having been capable of making the
claims he does in his reverie on Greek art?

Certainly, one possibility, as Margaret Rose argues when she
comes to her assessment of Marx's (not Heine's) reverie, lies
in Marx simply showing how historically uneven development
happens. The important thing is that Marx demonstrates in his
reverie the superiority of a decidedly materialist reading of
history and, thus, raises historical understanding as such to
a "higher level." In other words, it is historical understanding
itself that Marx means to elevate.[24] As I argue, though, Marx
less explains the general formulation of the contradiction he initially specifies (that there can be a form of social practice more

advanced than the conditions that give rise to it) than, in selecting and critically exploring the example par excellence (Greek art), discovers a new contradiction, that of the *appeal* of the unattainable norm and of the discordance of time that seems to come with it. Whatever it was that moved Greek society—it was a time founded on slavery, on myth, and on certain practices of government and commodity exchange, Marx notes—something leapt out of it that was beyond its own motions. On its very face, it appears that a social practice that barely made sense in its own time—*this itself* having appeal—reaches out to us out across time and space, although we must be highly circumspect in answering its call—this itself *also* appealing. It is a charm, Marx thinks. His affinity with and affection for this charm compel attention. If allowed, they also drop into the space that opens up between Marx's other value-voices.

So how does the charm work? What can it do? What does it say? The task is to bring the new contradiction signaled by this charm into the continuing exploration of the problem of value—the problem, that is, of finding the limit point of social forms (how social forms cease to represent social process) and regarding this limit point and the production thereof as essential, desirable social activity. It might be best to start by naming some of the affinities between Greek art and value, though, for I have left implicit that in Marx's handling of the subject, it is within value discourse (a value trope) at all. What is value-like about Marx's approach to Greek art? The established tropes already say. Though it was not a commodity worth another commodity as measured by average labor time equivalents, Marx thinks of Greek art as a form that represents the potential universality of human being and human practice.[25] That is, he assigns this art, however problematically, to the childhood of humanity but also posits it as a historically continuing norm—and so it verges on being a sort of exchange value, a measure across time, if you will. Of course, he immediately troubles these thoughts, too. In Marx's estimation, Greek society does not directly correspond to this art form and cannot be represented by it in any seamless, direct way. Instead, Greek art differentiates itself from Greek society. But right here Greek art is nudged further into the "concept of the value relation," for money owes its own special quality to its differentiation from all other things that matter—namely, other commodities (per the very next chapter of the *Grundrisse*, as well as the first volume of *Capital*). This is not to push Greek art back into commodity status after all but only to note that it and money are for Marx the centrally differentiated forms of their respective societies. No less, money, like Greek art, fails to be an adequate form of manifest social substance. Finally, the quantity/quality question that haunts the conventional term of value haunts Greek art, too. Where money is qualitatively boundless but quantitatively bounded, Marx would impose a qualitative boundary for Greek art because of the threat of its quantitative boundlessness (i.e., the propensity for it to be imitated). Greek art can be seen as the reverse of the money coin.

This is all to say that the significance of this art is grasped precisely through Marx's epistemology of value form. It seems to me, though, that the trope of value now appears with its own difference. For, Marx says, we are confronting a form that qualitatively exceeded the conditions of its production and that although relevant to the future (Greek art is a norm), also is off-limits to the future (Greek art is an unattainable norm). Marx sees the potential for (and disapproves of) its being slavishly copied, though as an art form it cannot immediately represent human universality in Marx's time nor in the future. If the past conditions during which this form was produced were to return (they cannot, Marx says), thus raising the possibility that as a norm it ought to be produced once more, it would not be these conditions per se that would be used to create this art anyway. For Marx, this is an art that *exceeded* its conditions. Note that Marx's evaluation is made doubly possible by his partial acceptance of his aesthetic milieu and by his having broken with the Hegelian conception of historical time, which saw time as structured by a succession of internally coherent periods.[26] Greek art existed in a state of discord at the time of its creation, remains in discord in Marx's time, and, Marx would say, will remain in discord in the time to come. *And these are the reasons why this form putatively charms us.* But talk about throwing down the gauntlet. Marx would have the truth of this art *developed* at a higher level. So what is the nature of this truth Marx is seizing on? There are several possibilities.

One, just seen, is that history needs to be understood as developing unevenly. Another is Marx's feeling that modern artists no longer need mythology as muse. Marx notes that Greek society was not a society "demanding from the artist an imagination independent of mythology" (150). Modern artists are free, however, to take modern understandings of nature and society as grist for aesthetic production. At the same time, art is, as a category and a sphere of social practice, subject to change in itself. New constellations of social practice (changing modes of production) can make something different of art. Just as Marx notices that art, per se, did not always exist—"certain branches of art, e.g. epos [epic], can no longer be produced in their epoch-making classic form *after artistic production as such has begun*" (149; emphasis added)—it is possible that its existence could change utterly later. Perhaps, art may no longer exist as a discrete practice in the future. But this, despite some wisdom, does not seem to be what Marx has in mind.[27] If anything, art should ramify: more people in the society of associated producers ought to be able to practice art. "Art" in some sense must survive.[28] Yet if art is also a sort of placeholder for production in the realm of freedom, why should people not produce as they please, including simulating Greek art? Not so good, Marx thinks. But why? Jacques Rancière calls this Marx's fear of "bastardy" and suggests that Marx never reconciles himself to that fear. That is, if Marx is interested in overturning Plato's idea that each performs what he is good at, by positing a time of associated labor when each might become good at many pursuits, Rancière also reads a Marx suspicious of copies. "Bastardy is the bad figure of Two," Rancière cryptically writes.

> That which does not split itself apart but contents itself
> with its duplication—as if it found, in the mixture that
> constitutes its indignity, strength to survive in escaping
> the fire of contradiction. The baseness of this history is
> its false nobility: its mixture of art and craftsmanship,

fabrication and imitation, usefulness and leisure, base and precious metals. Bastardy is as much the skill of the copper workers of old Nuremburg, who perfected a way of imitating goldwork, as it is the triviality of the worker-philosopher Proudhon, who desires useful works of art. For his own part, Doctor Marx is in favor of separation.[29]

But Marx is not simply in favor of separation. Rather, he seizes upon this as a subject of intense interest. What do we do, Marx wonders, about the desire to further *develop* certain aesthetic norms while *retaining* the appeal of art objects we would thereby refuse to copy?[30] The point is not simply to make an artsy thing, for even the Nazarenes of Marx's time could do this. The point is to produce an opening for the difference and disjuncture between a thing and its time to shine through. In sum, Marx finds a thingly example that actually surpasses its naïve quality and becomes norm; further, it surpasses its quality as norm and becomes unattainable. In this analysis "art" survives, Greek art at that, including a Greek art that survives our possible, illegitimate desire to copy it. It seems that Marx is in favor of separation not only between an artwork and its copy but between an artwork and everything else. We are indeed at the gates of a truth that is to be developed and we are invited to follow Marx and his object through them.

I can think of only one "truth" that Marx has in mind, and this concerns the disjunction itself between art and the other contemporary social practices. But look at how he also fights against this (if that is at all the right way to put it)! If Marx notes that Greek society because of its primitive technics did not need its artists to get beyond myth as a way of expressing their (and society's) understanding of the forces at work in the world and if he contrasts primitive understandings of forces with those understandings that underlie the development of the modern printing press, the railway, and the electric telegraph (not to mention the Internet, the airplane, and electronic publishing) *and* if he castigates the idea of copying Greek forms in the age of modern comprehension (why copy Greek art if there is no longer a need to send messages by marathon runners?), isn't part of him saying that modern artists ought to act in accordance with their times? Perhaps so. It is an indeterminate point to some degree. But if Marx is not saying quite this, which gives credence to Althusser's and to Trotsky's views of the semi-autonomous place of literature and the arts in society,[31] then the focus must be on the disjunction that is a constitutive part of Marx's analysis: differential development and differential times in (Greek) society and the objectification this gives rise to.

So let me return to the likeness between Greek art and money—that is, to the value discourse that is one way of reading this third scene. On the one hand, money in the commodity society is ultimately rendered limited by the very social processes that it sets in motion. It is entirely too fixed a form to handle the fluidity and chaos of actual commodity production and exchange, even though as a putative measure and a bearer of value, it ideally represents production and exchange and their spreading influence in the world. With Greek art, on the other hand, the relation to the form of universality is turned upside down. For Marx, Greek art renders limited the society that gave birth to it and does so in two senses. We cannot account for this art through a dissection of Greek society, while this art's mere existence exposes Greek society as comparatively less developed than its own art. I hasten to add that in reading Marx, Greek art is not seen for what it is (whatever that could mean anyway). It is seen hermeneutically as a thought Marx has, that it is good to engage in activities and produce objectified forms of these activities that expose the backwardness of conditions as they are, a backwardness that is immanent to the situation— until this art is produced, we do not know about the temporal disjuncture. (To give Marx's view of the key to the past a little turn, social individuals must actively produce the past that is the key to the future.) Like money, these art forms fail to represent the breadth of social processes, but unlike money, this is what marks their success, intended or not. In this light, we might imagine Marx wishing to see this upside-down role of art turned into an aspiration for the future in a society, putatively producing freely.[32]

Conclusion

In what remains I try to specify what such an aspiration could consist of, casting a backward glance toward the book's primary theme of value as a noncoalescing theory. I present these thoughts in no way as a program and, still less, as a blueprint but as touchstones for a social-political imaginary whose provocation is the value relation as a set of disjunctures with which Marx seems so taken—or so I read him.

Such an imaginary concerns, *first*, the relationship between the dominant means and forces of production in society and a social practice that denies these means a fully determinant function throughout society. In the case at hand, what Marx asserts about Greek art is that it gave the lie to contemporaneous means and forces of production as a limit to what this art might become. (Therefore, Marx's assumption, noted in part 2 of this book, that means and forces of production would keep pace with production that is truly free in a society of associated producers *must be suspended* here as a desideratum.) But what Marx also insists upon is, if we read him reading Greek art correctly, that played out over time and space, transformations of means and forces of production give the lie to any particular (art) form claiming to have durably exceeded those means and forces. Greek art eluded the productive milieu of Vulcan, Jupiter, and Hermes, as Marx puts it, but there is no meaning in modern art eluding these figures' grasp—productive forces have moved on. (This does not foreclose the possibility, mind you, that Marx's Greek reflections can be worked up as a guide for a proper critical appreciation of past—qua past—art and literature, if that is desired.)[33] Art, in its semiautonomy, cannot rest: the background to which it is articulated, the frame that makes art's semiautonomy a matter of relevance, is itself a moving quality. "Art," which I am of course compelled to place in scare quotes, is presented with new materials, ideas, skills, and questions, which are not of its making but which are nonetheless encountered by it. Thus, the art of producing surplus possibilities finds its limit in a sphere, which is, after all, also dynamic and not reducible to any particular, achieved form. Practices of surplus possibility (art) and the prevailing means/forces of production each present to the other a potential to be other than what they are. The relationship is dynamic, fraught, and multidirectional. For productive forces to keep up is not exactly the goal if disjuncture is what is sought or if, better put, we are going to let Marx keep his affective relationship to disjuncture, let alone our own.

Now, the *second* point is that this sort of affective relationship is not at all an easy task, so often do our affections run the other way. Consider Terry Eagleton's analysis of Marx's theory of Greek art. Eagleton correctly draws a connecting line between what Marx finds aesthetically agreeable about Greek art and the task he assigns the proletariat in the *Eighteenth Brumaire*—to write the "poetry of the future." Such poetry in the society of associated producers is for Eagleton's Marx a practice of self-exceeding.

> It is not simply a matter of discovering the expressive or representational forms "adequate to" the content of socialist revolution. It is a question of rethinking that opposition—of grasping form no longer as the symbolic mold into which content is poured, but as the "form of the content": which is to say, grasping form as the structure of a ceaseless self-production, and so not as "structure" but as "structuration." It is this process of continual self-excess—of the "content go(ing) beyond the phrase"—which is for Marx the poetry of the future and the sign of communism.[34]

But insofar as "form of the content" might smack of the self-knowing communists of the second scene I reconstruct—that is, the communism that knows itself—I do not think Eagleton plunges deep enough into the peculiar nature of Marx's gloss on Greek art. For what I am arguing here is that one of the meanings of Marx's comments on the higher development of the magic of Greek art is that the moment of self-exceeding does not come. It is delayed, strived for but not achieved; it too is suspended, and the something that is "art" is thrown out ahead of it, exceeding Eagleton's exceeded selves. And this is a moment of ironic pleasure, the charm Marx finds. Furthermore, this is not a moment that can be dissolved back into society, back into our experience of the world, since the nature of the charm would be to cast a light on what is limited about our experience. To not see this would be to plunge into ideology. Consider Eagleton's following closing statement:

> Once emancipated from material scarcity, liberated from labor, they [people] will live in the play of their mutual significations, move in the ceaseless "excess" of freedom. In that process, the signs of sense and value by which previous societies have lived their life-conditions will still, no doubt, be relevant. Yet if Marxism has maintained a certain silence about aesthetic value, it may well be because the material conditions which would make such discourse fully possible do not as yet exist.[35]

In my reading of Marx, though, these sorts of material conditions (i.e., those in which we imagine ourselves emancipated) must be made to *not* exist—they only would show us a false liberation. Thus, rare as it is, Marx's speech about aesthetic value and its development to a higher stage denies that content should overcome form, to use Eagleton's words, anymore than form should overcome content. Their disjuncture is more radical than that.

It seems to me that Greek art's appeal to Marx is the very particular way it manifested the surplus possibilities of its milieu as irredeemable surplus—this would be a *third* point. The more advanced nature of Greek art relative to its time opens a gap that cannot ever be closed: it has the paradoxical quality of being irrevocably out of synch with its times in such a way as is relevant only *to the time of the Greeks*. I am also saying then, with Marx egging us on toward a higher level, that in a society of associated producers in which producers reveal to each other and themselves the nature of the ties that bind them and, therefore, really live their social relation, as Marx says elsewhere, art would have a similar critical function and lend itself to the destabilizing of how social relations are "really" lived. So if Marx did not just illustrate the principle of uneven development but rendered the charms of uneven development as (a) value, a good society would be one that gives the lie to itself, that goes in search of its limit (its measure) *in its way*, specific to its time.

But this giving of the lie immediately poses new problems. Means and forces of production, despite what is imaginable or wanted, do not automatically necessitate a particular practice (art) emerging—this practice being *relatively* free to emerge on its own. Furthermore, the ongoing transformation of these means and forces ultimately necessitates that such a practice, if established as Marx indicates, be carried out differently in the future. This therefore means—here a *fourth* point—not only that the disjunction and discord is itself dynamic but that "art" is always pitched between nonnecessity and necessity. By this I imply that Greek art is not a representation to be replicated (Marx's preference for the Hellene over the Nazarene is relative, not absolute) but a process to be invented, a process that calls for invention, and invention of a specific kind. To hark back to Marx's letter to Kugelmann and explore its own possible unsaid (and why not also hark back to Foucault's heterotopias here, as well?), Marx's affinity for the charm of Greek art—the value form of Greek art, art as value form—signals the time and space taken that might be capable of illuminating the contours and confinements, the limits, of the other times and spaces of social production without substituting for them—Greek art does not throw its society into chaos—but showing them just the same that it is possible to be otherwise. (Would it be reasonable to propose that Marx's *Critique of the Gotha Program* plays Greek art to the Gotha socialists?)

The irony of course is that making this otherwise evident is an objectifying process itself. It involves the production of new forms that in being out of synch, are inassimilable surplus from the get-go and always have this status, this charm, and it involves the spur to eventually see these forms themselves as limits and so to reinvent them. Put differently, in associated production art would not take part in a general process of disalienation but—here is my *fifth* point—would knowingly attempt to produce moments of alienation, moments during which people and relations among them are not confirmed by the art object but dislocated and disoriented.[36] It is crucial that Marx regards Greek art as particular to the knowledge and understanding of the physical world of its time. Its producers were in that sense part of their worlds and its "mythological" perspective, as Marx terms it. But the quality of this art was such as to be out of synch with how mythological knowledge/understanding otherwise circulated. It signals the possibility of there always being another understanding, another knowledge, another shape that the world can have, even after everything else has been accounted for. What I take from Marx's note on Greek art is that we will not properly have this alternative(s) unless value becomes "an even higher law." That is, it is precisely when associated producers think they've solved the value problem that the value function of Greek art becomes most important and useful, as if to say that Marx has shown the desirability of developing the independent power (née "money") to a higher level. The truth about Greek art that is to be developed thus concerns the idea that our truth actually is, from this perspective, outside ourselves.

Is it possible for art to have this power or to assign such a power to art, since I believe this amounts to the same? Is it possible to choose to have a relationship with that which is inassimilable? Perhaps, it is only a matter of whether this is desired and put into practice. But perhaps, too, it is a matter of whether a society of associated producers could afford otherwise. If, as I earlier read Marx, value as social labor time does not disappear with capitalism but becomes an even more prominent, because decided ahead of time, feature of a society to come, there must be some element or moment, itself prized, through which to welcome the recognition of discordant time and space. If a nonutopian postcapitalism is more necessary than ever, it seems to me that such a position cannot be done without.

But what an immense difficulty we face in imagining a sine qua non role for a practice that is, today, so marginalized and reified, on the one hand, yet ubiquitous and fluid, on the other.

For today "art" is at once nowhere and everywhere. (Easier perhaps is to trace the prominent and active role for artistic production when it is yoked to nationalist or imperial fervor, noted already in conjunction with Marx's *Eighteenth Brumaire*.)[37] Temporality too has changed. Does Marx's nomenclature still work with its talk of the cultural pinnacles? Of the primitive? Of the advanced? Obviously not. But—to mark a *sixth* point—I do think that at a minimum it is necessary to imagine, with respect to art, a hunger that is as strong as our hunger for food, our yearning for friendship and love, for place and belonging, for sleep, for dreams, for change and movement—these are desires so deep that our bodies and minds seem to incline toward these desired objects as if of their own accord. Without these familiar hungers and the means by which to extend and enrich them, life is not life. As Marx notes elsewhere in the introduction to the *Grundrisse*, "hunger is hunger, but the hunger gratified by cooked meat eaten with a knife and fork is a different hunger from that which bolts down raw meat with the aid of hand, nail, and tooth." While I am bracketing the question of how much the nature of our desire can be apparent to us, as opposed to eluding us somewhere in our psyches, even after the illusions of the commodity have been shed, Marx's characterization of hunger tells us that there is no universal answer to how desires might identify their objects. It also tells us there is no one kind of object of desire. And because Marx posits no end to the becoming of species being, we can imagine that desire itself has no end, no ultimate satisfaction. Indeed, Marx's interest is in the increase of desire and of need, not capitalistically through the power of money and what it can buy and not through the constant exchange of one commodity for another but through the awakening of our senses through real sensual contact with the world. What this can mean for artistic and aesthetic production in a postcapitalist future perhaps is a question advantageously posed to those engaged in such activities now (even if what art would be in a later period might be quite different). How does working with paint and brush become a hunger that cannot be done without? What is it like to yearn deeply for clay, plaster, stone, wood, fiber, or a constellation of pixels? What reverberates in the body and mind when a new shape is brought forth? What do these or any other materials that are worked on require of the body and mind that works on them, and how is this in turn converted into a desperate hunger? Do musicians shiver with their music? Do they harbor unquenchable desires in their fingers for wire and wood, for ivory keys, for the tightly drawn skin of a drum? What is it like to feel an empty space between the neck and chin when the violin is not there? Is there a longing for the resistance of a bow as it's pulled and pushed across strings? Does the arm feel strange and limp when it's not draped over the body of a guitar, a sitar, or an oud? Is the only solution for the arm's hunger to play more? One has only to multiply the questions in accordance with the multiplication of aesthetic desire throughout a population to then begin making the link to how individuals could come to think of themselves as completely and utterly different from how they think of themselves now and of the role played by "objective" aesthetic experience (and the things that embody it) in producing the sense of dislocations, the sense that the conditions that seem to support them are actually being outlived and exceeded and that some new necessity is being called forth, giving rise to forms that cannot themselves be consumed through use and which defines their charm.[38]

In Marx's universe the essence of any being, any entity, lies outside itself. Its truth is what it can interact with, what it can change and how it can be changed in interaction. Its essence is, which interpreters as varied as Althusser and Deleuze and Guattari are eager to point out, that it lacks essence. In the case of the human species being, for example, we have a being who must, with the participation of the world, make its world. We do this through what Marx in those manuscripts from 1844 calls real sensuous activity that involves all our senses, itself taking the whole of human history to accomplish. This labor is understood relationally; it is, in the *Grundrisse*, "the form-giving fire, the transitoriness of things." In other words, labor is not activity in and of itself. It is the transformations it makes in the world, and it is the world acting back upon labor by demanding it be focused, attentive, adaptable.[39] This is an activity that confirms

not so much our being as our need to be *active* beings in order to be beings at all.[40] For Marx there is no being as such
beforehand—that is, before being active. Nothing can escape
this always-already original position and its repetition. In the
commodity society, the same truth necessarily holds. On the first
page of *Capital*, Marx's first analytical point about the commodity is that "in the first place" it is a thing outside us (and that as
a material its use can always be otherwise). The commodity
being on the outside and, thus, having a certain power over us
as residents of the commodity society means we are forced to
cede important powers to it: only by making and distributing
commodity things can arrangements among people emerge.
Our social life in the commodity society is thereby embedded in
and ruled by things: charms obviously take many kinds of form.

Until we grapple with Marx's discourse on Greek art as a
value, though, we might be tempted to read the immanence of
species being as a smooth, perfectible space in the future, the
tying together of essence and appearance as experienced by
those French communist workmen for whom smoking, drink-
ing, conversation, and brotherhood are enough. That at least
is one reading of Marx's well-rounded individuals to come and
no less one possible reading of his letter to Kugelmann: social
labor as essence finally actually appears rather than being the
essence mediated by the money-thing, which instead appears.
Such a finality is disrupted, however, by the point made a moment ago: the necessity to reckon with the objectified forms of
social labor.[41] It makes great sense, therefore, to start thinking
once again about the revalorization of reification or to experiment with the production of communist objects.[42] In what direc
tion might these recent gestures toward the inevitability that
human labor presents itself in fixities go? In reading the concept
of the value relation as multivocal, discordant, and given to in-
commensurabilities, I want—as a *seventh* point—to ask how to
pay respect to this idea of being ruled by things rather than considering this rule outmoded.[43] It should not escape our notice,
certainly not in the scenes in which my arguments are invested,
that Marx builds an analysis around *persisting* to cede a certain
power to things. To rehearse again, it should not surprise us that

a Rothschild would frame a bank note, and Marx's comment on this (itself a display) is predictable given the familiar way in which he is read. It is a more intriguing move when he lionizes the reflective quality of the work-hardened body, but there he reintroduces the problematic schisms we have seen elsewhere. The scene of Greek art is thoroughly destabilizing. Its power is about letting a thing speak to us in a fresh and new, and foreign, way as we welcome the lie it reveals about our world and any future world. While Marx in a sense is captive to a frame of mind that accepts the norms of high culture, from another perspective Greek art is full of objects that break open his usual view of our relation to things and give him something new to say and think about them. I want to see this for what I think it is. For what is it but the practice of a fetish?

In commodity production the social relation between things predicates social relations among people. Marx begs the question for associated production and allows us the idea of an art object that would throw into question the fullness and transparency of the social relations that people have determined for themselves—the radical gesture that a new Greek art might repredicate social relations, placing their nonplenary quality as much as possible in full view. Marx never gives up on the idea that the labor of making art is indeed productive labor, no matter what the bourgeois economists think. The labor of Greek art shows that humans are capable of producing things or revealing worldly qualities that unsettle the very understandings, habits, practices, and relations that are their milieu; that matter can be revealed that is beyond intention. Such production, whether it is an actual thing, a perception, a desire, or an inscription (I refrain from certainty), is what could stand between Marx's two voices when describing his beloved communist workmen. Marx sees in this group an element of pure, immanent becoming, a communism that "knows itself," as he writes of the communards during the Paris Commune,[44] and yet inscribes a need to take their measure, a need that seems built right into the very notion of what it means to value at all, as David Clarke argues in a brilliant essay on the limits to value.[45] "Greek art," whatever that could come concretely to mean, wedges itself between each of these valences, which threaten to unite in the single assertion that the measure has been fully taken, and cannily pulls the rug out from under. The truth of the outside is not then that of a plan brought to fruition, of objects that confirm the intentions of the acts behind them, but of an activity that produces *objective* surprises, twists, seductions, that produces forms that would really affect us, hail us into their space, and lure us into discovery of discord. (The distinction comes to mind between the mere "spirit *in* matter" and the more profound "spirit *of* matter" that Peter Pels makes in his important essay on the fetish.)[46] Herein maybe is the more enigmatic quality of the fetish though: that it cannot really be planned for—we summon it through observation, through critique, through new examinations and orientations. The new fetish would not be the property of individuals and would not monopolize the way in which things act on behalf of socially related people (as in the commodity society) but would be an art for which prevailing social relations could not account. Indeed, the reverse would be true: this art would call these social relations and their productive force into account. It would call them into question and ask them to be reinventive, taking away the sense of completion and giving a desired sense of absence in return. "Greek art," in other words is a quality, a singularity produced in the course of social production but not a reflection or representation of the social formation "whose" revelation it is. To paraphrase Marx's well-worn gloss on labor power, social production might create or reveal something in excess of what it itself is, a reflection of its shortcoming, an underdetermined result.

Yet a *final* gambit is ventured: that what all of this points to is in excess of excess. For I think this is what it comes down to if Marx's implied reconstruction of the fetish has any sway. Consider his thinly formulated but wonderfully portentous statement about the unity of art and the public. "The object of art," he writes, "like every other product—creates a public which is sensitive to art and enjoys beauty."[47] But what are these affinities if the object of art *need not immediately create its public*? Greek art, as with Marx's refutation of Say's law—that production equals consumption denies such an immediate identity.

This question does indeed answer itself. Earlier, I write of Marx's two voices when describing the satisfactions and pleasures of those communist workmen in what I dub the second scene. I argue for the necessity of some, let's say, principle that would keep these voices from collapsing into each other. I read the charm of Greek art as such a principle objectified, as a form of value that adds to the two voicings Marx speaks in the second scene by serving as a third voice that interpellates a public to come, a people in a Greek art relation to themselves, persisting with the unattainable. This new form of value does not deny accounting for needs or the coming of new needs, does not deny our pleasures and surpluses—our drink, our conversation, our bodily pleasure—but stands as a differential of that surplus and intensifies the agonistic politics that these multivocal conceptions of value might inspire. Greek art in Marx's reading was thrown outside of the Greeks; it neither denied nor confirmed their needs and their pleasures, but in seeing this art, Marx discerns the contours and limits of that social formation. Any future worth having would have its own Greek art and its own capacity to be charmed by it. As a quality differentiated from the ordinary metabolism of social and individual becoming—the ordinary metabolism implied in Marx's letter to Kugelmann—it is like a meal that cannot or dare not be eaten, an offering made by people to themselves, learning to hunger for hunger itself, or like an organ without a body.

Notes

Introduction

1. Marx, "Economic and Philosophic Manuscripts of 1844," 105.

2. For a recent treatment of these classic conundrums of value theory, see Freeman et al., *The Value Controversy*. Elson, "The Value Theory of Labor," also has an excellent overview.

3. Harvie, "All Labor Produces Value for Capital," concords well with Diane Elson's treatment of value in "The Value Theory of Labor." Note the spelling difference from David Harvey.

4. Arthur, *The New Dialectics*; Althusser and Balibar, *Reading "Capital"*; Karatani, *Transcritique*; Gidwani, *Capital, Interrupted*; Deleuze and Guattari, *Anti-Oedipus*; Hardt and Negri, *Multitude*; Casarino, "Marx before Spinoza."

5. On this point see Castree, "On Theory's Subject."

6. For the immature and mature Marx, see Postone, *Time, Labor, and Social Domination*. For the early and late Marx, see Althusser and Balibar, *Reading "Capital."*

7. Jameson, *Representing Capital*, 1–46.

8. Gidwani, *Capital, Interrupted*.

9. For example, both refutation and conflation appear in Postone, *Time, Labor, and Social Domination*.

10. Graeber, *Toward an Anthropological Theory of Value*; cf. De Angelis, "Value(s), Measure(s) and Disciplinary Markets"; cf. Miller, "The Uses of Value."

1. The Value–Capital Couplet and How to Break It

1. In addition to the complexities of value that make it difficult to think, it also is the case that the value concept is not a given in the history of economic theory. That is, value as a concern in economic thought waxes and wanes. It is not of transhistorical importance. See Jorland, "The Coming into Being and Passing Away of Value Theories," for example, on the history of value theories as such.

2. Spivak, "Scattered Speculations on the Question of Value," is

a widely read interrogation of how value seizes on these matters of theory versus history. See also the lucid and instructive essays of Noel Castree, "Birds, Mice and Geography" and "Invisible Leviathan." Joseph Fracchia, "Marx's *Aufhebung* of Philosophy and the Foundation of a Materialist Science of History," sketches out the tension between Marx as theoretician and as historian through a reading of the chronological development of Marx's thought. See also Althusser, "Marx in His Limits," a posthumously published essay on the many unspoken and unacknowledged assumptions of Marx's arguments. The tension between theory and empirics is not the only vexation. It is a problem, of which most of the authors just cited are aware, that Marx's thought and writing is the site of different theoretical frameworks that are difficult to reconcile. As one example of some very interesting recent discussion along these lines, see the work of Andrew Brown, "Developing Realistic Philosophy" and "A Materialist Development of Some Recent Contributions to the Labor Theory of Value," on the realist and dialectical strains in Marxist philosophy.

3. A preeminent argument that refuses to accept that capitalism is totalizing is Gibson-Graham, *The End of Capitalism (As We Knew It)*; cf. Gibson-Graham, *A Postcapitalist Politics*. Similar stakes, especially the question of whether capitalist (or simply market) value systems work by necessarily bracketing off and disavowing the world's social and natural complexity or even more fundamentally are themselves internally constituted through noneconomic practices, are played out in Callon, ed., *The Laws of the Markets*; Miller and Carrier, eds., *Virtualism*; and Miller, "Turning Callon the Right Way Up." See also Massey, "Economic: Non-economic."

4. For example, see Weeks, "Feminist Standpoint Theories and the Return of Labor."

5. Arthur, *The New Dialectics*, is a representative example. Althusser, "Marx in His Limits," pins this problem on Marx feeling obligated to adopt a certain conception of science (Hegelian) that requires beginning with abstraction rather than the concrete (39–43). That Marx could break with this method as the writing of *Capital* wore on is proof to Althusser that Marx is at root a thinker of overdetermined causation—Marx's failure *is* his success, Althusser asserts.

6. These points, that abstract labor is obvious and yet also produced unawares, are made in Marx, *Capital*, vol. 1., 163–64, 166–67.

7. Clarke, "The Seduction of Space," 70. For this particular point, Clarke draws upon Metz, "Photography and Fetish."

8. Bauman, "Understanding as the Work of History," 59.

9. I am painfully aware that this sort of intentionality with regard to economic affairs is scarred deeply by the historical experience of centralized planning, which gives credence to the view that there is simply no alternative to capitalism. Nonetheless, the political field remains vibrant with a refusal to accept this view, as even a few cogent examples demonstrate. See the discussions of Elson, "Market Socialism or Socialization of Markets" and "Socializing Markets, Not Market Socialism"; Dyer-Witherford, *Cyber-Marx*; and the special issue "The New Cooperativism" of the journal *Affinities*.

10. While it might seem to be splitting hairs, the foregoing discussion means I disagree with De Angelis, "Social Relations, Commodity-Fetishism, and Marx's Critique of Political Economy," in which he argues that Marx's theory of value is exclusively grounded in a theory of capital and that this theory grounds the concept of the commodity fetish. I argue, as Diane Elson in "Market Socialism" also does, that the commodity fetish, because it is a statement of what is wrong with an independent power materialized in things that exceed social consciousness, is necessary to understanding why capital is itself a problem. De Angelis himself is taking issue with Rubin, *Essays on Marx's Theory of Value*.

11. Harvey, *A Companion to Marx's "Capital,"* would be such a careful example.

12. Althusser, "Marx in His Limits," 129.

13. Castree, "Invisible Leviathan"; Spivak, "Scattered Speculations."

14. For a wide-ranging discussion of these themes, see, as just one example, Storper and Walker, *The Capitalist Imperative.*

15. Arthur, *The New Dialectics*; Murray, "Marx's 'Truly Social' Labor Theory of Value: Part I" and "Marx's 'Truly Social' . . . Part II."

16. Sheppard and Barnes have championed a disequilibrium approach to the concept of value—that is, the idea that insofar as value is a dynamic system, it is one that intrinsically tends toward multiple possible alternative (political economic) states. See Sheppard and Barnes, *The Capitalist Space Economy*; cf. Bergmann et al., "Capitalism beyond Harmonious Equilibrium."

17. Murray, "Marx's 'Truly Social' Labor Theory of Value: Part II," 102; cf. Roberts, "The Visible and the Measurable."

18. Murray, "Marx's 'Truly Social' Labor Theory of Value: Part II," 132. See also De Angelis, "Social Relations, Commodity Fetishism and Marx's Critique of Political Economy."

19. See Christopher Arthur's thoroughgoing development of the Hegel–Marx connection in *The New Dialectics.*

20. See Mosley, ed., *Marx's Method in "Capital."*
21. Doel, "Dialectical Materialism," 76.

2. The Politics of Capitalist "Totality" in a More-Than-Capitalist World

1. For Marx, C . . . M . . . C also generally describes the commodification and remuneration of labor power under the wage labor form of production. But I hope it is clear that this is a separate point.
2. See Marx, *Capital*, vol. 1, especially the footnotes on pages 161, 178–9, 181, and 188–89.
3. Rancière, *The Philosopher and His Poor*, 114. For an extended discussion of labor money schemes that concern Marx, see Saad-Filho, "Labor, Money, and Labor-Money." Alternative currency schemes continue to exist, plagued by some of the problems Marx identified long ago. But as North, *Money and Liberation*, shows, participants in these schemes do not always judge their desirability and worth exclusively on the grounds of economic rationality. Contra Marx, present-day alternative currencies might be acceptable less as bearers of value than as bearers or symbols of *values*, such as fidelity to locality and place, to the struggle against larger national or global scales of economic abstraction, to local production and consumption, and so on.
4. Holland, "Nonlinear Historical Materialism and Postmodern Marxism," picks up on this theme, arguing for the relevance of Marx to certain new forms of historical materialism that maintain an interest in markets but not capitalism (namely, the nonlinear materialism of Manuel De Landa).
5. This is a longtime fascination of Marx that appears in different guises and rhetorical flourishes. Thus, in a very different context and through a certain sort of wordplay, the very appearance of the Paris Commune, Marx writes in "The Civil War in France," is "its own measure," while also holding that it must take measures.
6. Cleaver, *Reading "Capital" Politically*, 112–17.
7. Ibid., 77–78.
8. Marx, *A Contribution to the Critique of Political Economy*, 213. The larger context is that Cleaver—and De Angelis, "Social Relations," to point to another example—is reacting against a long lineage, from Engels to Ronald Meek and beyond, that reads the first part of *Capital* as theorizing value exclusively in the form of precapitalist simple commodity production. See Engels, *Ludwig Feuerbach*, and Meek, *Economics and Ideology*. Obviously, Cleaver rejects this reading. Ar-

thur, "The Myth of Simple Commodity Production," traces the idea of simple commodity production back to Engels, who is (mistakenly) looking for a way to shore up Marx's labor theory of value against the concept of prices of production introduced in volume 3 of *Capital*. The issue for Engels is how to reconcile Marx's assumption in volume 1 that goods exchange at their values (i.e., prices directly express labor values) with Marx's relaxing that assumption in the drafts he prepared for volume 3. This indeed is a problem for value theorists of a certain kind who wonder about its explanatory potential in the real world of actual commodity flows and prices. See Harvey, *Limits to Capital*, chap. 2, for an excellent précis on the whole matter.

9. See Marx, *Grundrisse*, 137.

10. Ibid., 139–40.

11. Ibid., 143–4.

3. The End of Value (As We Know It)

1. Kliman, *Reclaiming Marx's "Capital."*

2. Diskin, "Rethinking Socialism," 292.

3. Sheppard and Barnes, *The Capitalist Space Economy*, 62–63, is very good on this point; see also Harvey, *Limits to Capital*.

4. It is Marx's business to *produce* such a need, as Lebowitz emphasizes in *Beyond "Capital,"* esp. chap. 10.

5. This particular break erupts at the end of chapter 49 in *Capital*, vol. 3, "On the Analysis of the Production Process." The chapter itself takes up the question of how the spending of revenues is made consistent (or not) with the necessity of reproducing the means of production. On the penultimate page, Marx readies the early nineteenth-century political economist Heinrich Storch for a dressing down. According to Marx (who provides a quote), Storch claims that political economy understands commodities on the basis of two norms, "values, in relation to individuals" and "goods, in relation to the nation." Storch seems to be searching for a way to justify both differences of individual fortune and some underlying foundation of needs to be met through the lens of how things rather than, say, time is distributed. Marx has none of it and, so, concludes the chapter: "Firstly, it is a false abstraction to treat a nation whose mode of production is based on value, and organized capitalistically into the bargain, as a unified body simply working for the national needs. Secondly, even after the capitalist mode of production is abolished, though social production remains, the determination of value still prevails in the sense that the regulation

of labor-time and the distribution of social labor among various production groups becomes more essential than ever, as well as the keeping accounts of this" (991). Though there are debates over how literally
to take Marx on this second point, it's quite clear that value and capital
are not reducible to each other and that associated production must
be thought in value terms. We saw a similar passage earlier in the present book in the *Grundrisse* in "The Chapter on Money." (Nota bene,
insofar as Marx indicates the law of value has a quantitative solution
that could be worked out only noncapitalistically—the necessity of
keeping accounts—this has given rise to some interesting discussions
that readers may want to consult. See, for example, Itoh, "Money and
Credit in Socialist Economies." As Trevor Barnes recently calls attention to, there is no point denying that Marx is, among other things, a
quantitative thinker. See Barnes, "Not Only . . . But Also.") In my view,
there is a consistency between Marx insisting on the presence of value
in associated production and what he describes as his critical "method
of political economy" in the *Grundrisse*. To wit, what bourgeois political economy takes to be universal categories (e.g., labor, money, population), Marx sees as taking on differential meaning in different societies, such that labor performed by slaves presumes slavery, whereas
labor performed by wage workers presumes capitalism. When Marx
remarks that the determination of value becomes even more important after capitalism than during it, is he not proposing that the value
concept in capital presumes capital and class as its basis, whereas
associated production after capital would presume value as its basis?
As I have already stated, this is not to say *real* value occurs in associated production; it is to say that value does not coalesce into a single
theory and, as I put it in the opening pages, splits along the fault line
of problem and solution. With this in mind, I differ from Harvie, who
suggests in "All Labor Produces Value" that forging the link between
labor and value is *capital's* problem.

    6. Sayers, "Creative Activity and Alienation in Hegel and Marx."

    7. Marx, *Grundrisse*, 611.

    8. Perhaps what will guarantee that production in the realm of
true freedom is that means of production will have remained social-
ized. But if this is a realm beyond compulsion, what will compel the
continuation of such production along social lines? Perhaps the answer is that in the society of associated producers the individuals will
be different; Marx says as much. But if this is so, they still must feel
that there is something essential about the social aspect of their individuality—that there is a real need fulfilled in that sphere. And there

we return to the problem again. Need is outside real freedom. It is the condition and basis for freedom, yes, but nonetheless outside the experience of freedom.

9. For a discussion of the implications and pitfalls of this assumption, see David Graeber's intriguing commentary in "The Sadness of Post-workerism."

4. From Necessity to Freedom and Back Again

1. Casarino, "Surplus Common," 15, and for the wider discussion, 15–36; cf. Lebowitz, *Beyond Capital*, chap. 11.

2. Read, "Figures of the Common." To be fair, I think Casarino might be sympathetic to my point, as in his equally remarkable concluding essay to *In Praise of the Common*, he considers the irreducible tension and traffic between pleasure and production (see especially 242–45), something that I regard as squarely a question of value. I do so insofar as pleasure and production loosely intertwine with notions of freedom and necessity, the vexed matter of measure that shuttles in between these notions, and on toward the question I sketch in chapter 5 of what a value-theoretic experience of pleasure might be like.

3. Of course, if as Marx writes in the first volume of *Capital*, nature does not make capital on one side and labor on the other, then what else would this law be but inner? It is worth remarking that Marx rarely refers to a law of value, as George Caffentzis points out in "Immeasurable Value?" Caffentzis's essay is interesting for other reasons, as well, being a critique of Hardt and Negri's notion that value, in the now *affective* stage of capitalist development, where the line between work and life blurs, is beyond measure. Against this idea Caffentzis offers an account of capital's increasing colonization of *time* in everyday life (cf. Harvie, "All Labor Produces Value"; Cleaver, "Work, Value, and Domination.")

4. See Marx, *Capital*, vol. 1, 476, for a passage that roughly parallels the one from volume 3 discussed here. Marx writes in that passage of the "inner relation" that arises spontaneously and whose value effect is a posteriori.

5. Marx has a long discussion in volume 3 of counteractions to the tendency of falling profit rates. None of these negate, however, the point I make here. These counteractions are worth paying attention to, though, as it is tempting to make too much of the falling profit rate as the primary dialectical strand of capitalism. Cf. Moishe Postone, *Time, Labor, and Social Domination*.

6. Postone, "Critique and Historical Transformation."
7. Cf. Mann, "Time, Space, and Money in Capitalism and Communism."
8. Marx, *Capital*, vol. 1, 231. On the Aristotle–Marx connection, see Casarino, *In Praise of the Common*.
9. In chapter 14 of the first volume of *Capital*, Marx refers to the labor of the working class as Sisyphus-like, the same metaphor previously chosen to describe the miser's labor.
10. Marx, *Grundrisse*, 222.
11. See Marx's analysis of the labor process in *Capital*, vol.1, 283–306.
12. He revises this view at the very end of the volume when he gets to a discussion of primitive accumulation (i.e., the violent preconditions for capitalism's spontaneous emergence: forcible removals of peoples, eradication of traditional resource rights, rules against vagabondage and loitering, and the whole sordid history that makes for the emergence of a working class).
13. Gorz, *Ecologica*.
14. Zygmunt Bauman draws this point out in the provocative short treatise *Freedom*, in which he claims freedom can be posited only from within a certain kind (read delimited and delimiting) of social relation.
15. Cf. Holland, "Spinoza and Marx," paragraph 21.

5. The Value Hypothesis

1. Marx, "Letter to Kugelmann," 524–25.
2. See Lenin's remarks on Marx's attitude toward the events that led to the Paris Commune, a revolt that Marx was at first set against. Lenin, "Preface to the Russian Translation of Karl Marx's Letters to Dr. Kugelmann."
3. Marx, *The German Ideology*, 56–57.
4. Hardt and Negri, *Commonwealth*, 319.
5. Jameson, *Representing "Capital."*
6. Marx, *Capital*, vol. 1, 279.
7. Marx, *Grundrisse*, 231.
8. Gidwani, *Capital, Interrupted*.
9. Marx, "Economic and Philosophic Manuscripts of 1844," 99–100.
10. Cf. Read, "The Production of Subjectivity: From Transindividuality to the Common."
11. Hardt and Negri, *Commonwealth*; cf. Cleaver, "The Inversion of Class Perspective."
12. Sayers, "Creative Activity and Alienation."
13. As Slavoj Žižek, who also is much taken with a process-oriented

ontology of subject formation, writes in his divination of Hegel's philosophy of spirit, "If the status of the subject is thoroughly 'processual,' it means that it emerges through the very failure to fully actualize itself." See Žižek, *Living in the End Times*, 232. If so, it is possible for the "processual" to produce and leave material traces of this failure that are not themselves failures but rather in excess of subjects. Can the processual produce something in excess of the subject? My discussion of Greek art later in the chapter bears this question in mind.

14. Deleuze and Guattari, *Anti-Oedipus*; cf. Read, "The Production of Subjectivity."

15. Marx, *Grundrisse*, 108; Althusser, "Contradiction and Overdetermination."

16. Gidwani, *Capital, Interrupted*. On capital's dependence upon the absolute exteriority of living labor, see Dussel, *The Four Drafts of "Capital."*

17. Althusser and Balibar, *Reading "Capital."* On the "last moment" that "never comes," see Althusser, "Contradiction and Overdetermination," 113.

18. "Human anatomy contains a key to the anatomy of the ape," Marx writes. "The intimations of higher development among the subordinate animal species, however, can be understood only after the higher development is already known." In like fashion, "the bourgeois economy thus supplies the key to the ancient, etc. But not at all in the manner of those economists who smudge over all historical differences." See Marx, *Grundrisse*, 105.

19. Rose, *Marx's Lost Aesthetic*.

20. Eagleton, "Marxism and Aesthetic Value," is the most cogent theoretical treatment that I know of on Marx's comments on Greek art in the *Grundrisse* and their relation to Marx's other writings. As I describe later, however, I do not fully agree with the conclusions he draws.

21. Harvey, *Paris, Capital of Modernity*.

22. Rose, *Marx's Lost Aesthetic*, 79–96.

23. Ibid., 20.

24. Ibid., 91.

25. I do not deny that ancient Greek art objects can be fictitious commodities, as is the case with our example of the Elgin Marbles. These objects, taken from the Parthenon, were purchased by the British government from Lord Elgin for display in the British Museum. Elgin had procured them in Athens from its Ottoman rulers.

26. Althusser and Balibar, *Reading "Capital."*

27. Lefebvre, *Critique of Everyday Life*, vol. 2.

28. Cf. Morawski, Introduction, 22. See also Alex Loftus's wonderful essays on Marxism, art, and urban political ecology in *Everyday Environmentalism*.

29. Rancière, *The Philosopher and His Poor*, 67.

30. Rancière recognizes this struggle in Marx, I think, without quite saying so. See his comments on Marx as artist in his approach to drafting the text for the *Critique of the Gotha Program*: Marx has more desire to produce a model document than he has faith in its being adopted. Posterity instead is Marx's aim, or so claims Rancière in *The Philosopher and His Poor*, 116–17.

31. Althusser repeatedly makes this point; see *Reading "Capital"*; Trotsky, *Literature and Revolution*.

32. In multiple writings, Marx explicitly and implicitly suggests a variety of roles that artistic production might play in a postcapitalist society. The inference that I draw from what I dub the scene of Greek art is only one. See the very useful selection and discussion in Baxandall and Morawski, *Marx and Engels on Literature and Art*.

33. See Macherey, *In a Materialist Way*.

34. Eagleton, "Marxism and Aesthetic Value," 184.

35. Ibid., 187.

36. See Morawski, Introduction, for a different view. For statements that are in high sympathy with Marx here, see Foucault, "What Is Enlightenment?," especially the characterization of Baudelaire's view of modern painting and Foucault's acceptance of this as an "attitude of modernity"; see also Althusser, "Creminini, Painter of the Abstract." That said, I do not think either Foucault or Althusser truly grab by the lapels Marx's central question about Greek Art and its appeal.

37. For a broader study of politics in an aesthetic key, see Sartwell, *Political Aesthetics*.

38. In setting down these thoughts, I am painfully aware of how precious I might be making art seem. Maybe art really is just a placeholder for production that is truly free (in the qualified sense conveyed here). But in consideration of the possibility that this temptation is itself symptomatic of how our needs under capitalism have become paltry and impoverished and perhaps symptomatic, too, of the historically liminal place of aesthetic experiences in Marxist theory, I have decided to let the example of art stand or fall on its own merits. Readers may take it for what it is worth. See Barrett, "The Place of Aesthetics in Marxist Criticism."

39. See *Grundrisse*, 612.

40. To contrast his views with Adam Smith's, Marx makes much of this point in the *Grundrisse* in the section on theories of surplus value. See *Grundrisse*, 610–12.

41. This is the perspective from which I read the contrast that David Harvey draws in *Spaces of Hope* between what he calls utopias of process and utopias of form.

42. On revalorizing reification, see Read, "The Production of Subjectivity"; Thoburn, "Communist Objects."

43. Although "the rule of things" is not the most apt phrase, there are the beginnings of some interesting conversations between the concept of value and new materialisms that grant a certain vitality to nonhuman matter. On the new materialisms, see Braun and Whatmore's superb edited collection *Political Matter*. The agency of matter, as it circulates through capital and staged as an encounter between Marx and Latour (actor networks), is a theme also taken up in Castree, "Marxism, Capitalism, and the Production of Nature" and "Nature, Economy, and the Cultural Politics of Theory"; Kirsch and Mitchell, "The Nature of Dead Things." Braun, "Toward a New Earth and a New Humanity," opts for a more-than-human account of capitalism that is Deleuzian in nature (i.e., emphasizing the open-ended becoming of matter).

44. Marx and Engels, *On the Paris Commune*.

45. Clarke, "The Limits to Value."

46. Pels, "The Spirit of Matter."

47. Marx, *Grundrisse*, 92.

Bibliography

Althusser, Louis. "Contradiction and Overdetermination." In *For Marx*, 89–128. New York: Vintage Books,1969.

———. "Creminini, Painter of the Abstract." In *Lenin and Philosophy and Other Essays*, 157–166. New York: Monthly Review Press, 2001.

———. "Marx in His Limits." In *Philosophy of the Encounter*, 7–162. New York: Verso, 2006.

Althusser, Louis, and Étienne Balibar. *Reading "Capital."* New York: Verso, 1998.

Arthur, Christopher J. *The New Dialectics and Marx's "Capital."* Boston: Brill, 2004.

———. "The Myth of Simple Commodity Production." In *Marx Myths and Legends*, edited by R. Lucas and A. Blunden. Marxmyths.org, 2005. http://marxmyths.org/chris-arthur/article2.htm.

Barnes, Trevor. "'Not Only . . . But Also': Quantitative and Critical Geography." *The Professional Geographer* 61, no. 3 (2009): 292–300.

Barrett, Michele. "The Place of Aesthetics in Marxist Criticism." In *Marxism and the Interpretation of Culture*, edited by Cary Nelson and Lawrence Grossberg, 697–713. Chicago: University of Illinois Press, 1988.

Bauman, Zygmunt. "Understanding as the Work of History: Karl Marx." In *Hermeneutics and Social Science*, 48–68. New York: Columbia University Press, 1978.

———. *Freedom.* Minneapolis: University of Minnesota Press, 1988.

Baxandall, Lee, and Stefan Morawski, eds. *Marx and Engels on Literature and Art: A Selection of Writings.* St. Louis, Mo.: Telos Press, 1973.

Bergmann, Luke, Eric Sheppard, and Paul Plummer. "Capitalism beyond Harmonious Equilibrium: Mathematics as if Human Agency Mattered." *Environment and Planning A* 41, no. 2 (2009): 265–83.

Braun, Bruce. "Toward a New Earth and a New Humanity." In *David Harvey: A Critical Reader*, edited by Noel Castree and Derek Gregory, 191–222. Oxford: Blackwell, 2006.

Braun, Bruce, and Sarah Whatmore, eds. *Political Matter.* Minneapolis: University of Minnesota Press, 2010.

Brown, Andrew. "Developing Realistic Philosophy: From Critical Realism to Materialist Dialectics." In *Critical Realism and Marxism*, edited by Andrew Brown, Steve Fleetwood, and John Michael Roberts, 168–86. New York: Routledge, 2002.

———. "A Materialist Development of Some Recent Contributions to the Labor Theory of Value." *Cambridge Journal of Economics* 32 (2008): 125–46.

Caffentzis, George. "Immeasurable Value? An Essay on Marx's Legacy." *The Commoner* 10 (Spring/Summer 2005): 87–114.

Callari, Antonio, and David Ruccio, eds. *Postmodern Materialism and the Future of Marxist Theory: Essays in the Althusserian Tradition.* Hanover, N.H.: Wesleyan University Press, 1996.

Callon, Michel, ed. *The Laws of the Markets.* Malden, Mass.: Blackwell, 1998.

Casarino, Cesare. *Modernity at Sea: Melville, Marx, Conrad in Crisis.* Minneapolis: University of Minnesota Press, 2002.

———. "Surplus Common: A Preface." In *In Praise of the Common*, edited by Cesare Casarino and Antonio Negri, 1–39. Minneapolis: University of Minnesota Press, 2008.

———. "Marx before Spinoza: Notes toward an Investigation." In *Spinoza Now*, edited by Dimitris Vardoulakis, 179–234. Minneapolis: University of Minnesota Press, 2011.

Casarino, Cesare, and Antonio Negri. *In Praise of the Common.* Minneapolis: University of Minnesota Press, 2008.

Castree, Noel. "On Theory's Subject and Subject's Theory: Harvey, Capital, and the Limits to Classical Marxism." *Environment and Planning A* 27 (1995): 269–97.

———. "Birds, Mice and Geography: Marxism and Dialectics." *Transactions of the Institute of British Geographers* 21, no. 2 (1996): 342–46.

———. "Invisible Leviathan: Speculations on Marx, Spivak, and the Question of Value." *Rethinking Marxism* 9, no. 2 (1996/97): 45–78.

———. "Nature, Economy and the Cultural Politics of Theory: The 'War against the Seals' in the Bering Sea, 1870–1911." *Geoforum* 28, no. 1(1997): 1–20.

———. "Marxism, Capitalism, and the Production of Nature." In *Social Nature*, edited by Bruce Braun and Noel Castree, 189–207. Malden, Mass.: Blackwell, 2001.

Clarke, David B. "The Limits to Value." In *The SAGE Handbook of*

Social Geographies, edited by Susan J. Smith, Rachel Pain, Sallie A. Marston, and John-Paul Jones III, 253–68. London: Sage, 2010.

———. "The Seductions of Space." In *Consuming Space: Placing Consumption in Perspective*, edited by Michael K. Goodman, David Goodman, and Michael Redclift, 57–77. Burlington, Vt.: Ashgate, 2010.

Cleaver, Harry. "The Inversion of Class Perspective in Marxian Theory: From Valorization to Self-Valorization." In *Open Marxism*, vol. 2, edited by Werner Bonefield, Richard Gunn, and Kosmas Psychopedis, 106–44. London: Pluto Press, 1992.

———. *Reading "Capital" Politically*. San Francisco: AK Press, 2000.

———. "Work, Value, and Domination." *The Commoner* 10 (Spring/Summer 2005): 115–31.

De Angelis, Massimo. "Social Relations, Commodity-Fetishism and Marx's Critique of Political Economy." *Review of Radical Political Economics* 28, no. 4 (1996): 1–29.

———. "Value(s), Measure(s) and Disciplinary Markets." *The Commoner* 10 (Spring/Summer 2005): 66–86.

Deleuze, Gilles, and Félix Guattari. *Anti-Oedipus*. Minneapolis: University of Minnesota Press, 1983.

Diskin, Jonathan. "Rethinking Socialism: What's in a Name?" In *Postmodern Materialism and the Future of Marxist Theory*, edited by Antonio Callari and David F. Ruccio, 278–99. London: Wesleyan University Press, 1996.

Doel, Marcus. "Dialectical Materialism: Stranger than Friction." In *David Harvey: A Critical Reader*, edited by Noel Castree and Derek Gregory, 55–79. Oxford: Blackwell, 2006.

Dussel, Enrique. "The Four Drafts of Capital: Toward a New Interpretation of the Dialectical Thought of Marx." *Rethinking Marxism* 13, no. 1 (2001): 10–26.

Dyer-Witherford, Nick. *Cyber-Marx: Cycles and Circuits of Struggle in High-Technology Capitalism*. Chicago: University of Illinois Press, 1999.

Eagleton, Terry. "Marxism and Aesthetic Value." In *Criticism and Ideology: A Study in Marxist Literary Theory*, 162–87. New York: Verso, 1998.

Elson, Diane. "The Value Theory of Labor." In *Value: The Representation of Labor in Capitalism*, edited by Diane Elson, 115–80. London: CSE Books, 1978.

———. "Market Socialism or Socialization of Markets?" *New Left Review* 172 (November/December 1988): 3–44.

———. "Socializing Markets, Not Market Socialism." *Socialist Register* 36 (2000): 67–85.

Engels, Friedrich. *Ludwig Feuerbach.* London: Lawrence and Wishart, 1906.

Foucault, Michel. *The Order of Things.* New York: Random House, 1970.

———. "What Is Enlightenment?" In *The Foucault Reader,* edited by Paul Rabinow, 32–50. New York: Pantheon Books, 1984.

Fracchia, Joseph. "Marx's *Aufhebung* of Philosophy and the Foundations of a Materialist Science of History." *History and Theory* 30, no. 2 (1991): 153–79.

Freeman, Alan, Andrew Kliman, and Julian Wells, eds. *The Value Controversy and the Foundation of Economics.* Cheltenham, UK: Edward Elger, 2004.

Gibson-Graham, J. K. *The End of Capitalism (As We Knew It).* Minneapolis: University of Minnesota Press, 2006.

———. *A Postcapitalist Politics.* Minneapolis: University of Minnesota Press, 2006.

Gidwani, Vinay. *Capital, Interrupted.* Minneapolis: University of Minnesota Press, 2008.

Gorz, André. *Ecologica.* London: Seagull Books, 2010.

Graeber, David. *Toward an Anthropological Theory of Value: The False Coin of Our Own Dreams.* New York: Palgrave, 2001.

———. "The Sadness of Post-workerism." *The Commoner* website. April 1, 2008. http://www.commoner.org.uk/?p=33.

Hardt, Michael, and Antonio Negri. *Multitude.* New York: Penguin, 2004.

———. *Commonwealth.* Cambridge: Harvard University Press, 2009.

Harvey, David. *The Limits to Capital.* Oxford: Basil Blackwell, 1982.

———. *Spaces of Hope.* Berkeley: University of California Press, 2000.

———. *Paris, Capital of Modernity.* New York: Routledge, 2003.

———. *A Companion to Marx's "Capital."* New York: Verso, 2010.

Harvie, David. "All Labor Produces Value for Capital and We All Struggle against Value." *The Commoner* 10 (Spring/Summer 2005): 132–71.

Holland, Eugene. "Spinoza and Marx." *Cultural Logic* 2, no. 1 (1998). eserver.org/clogic/2-1/Holland.html.

———. "Nonlinear Historical Materialism and Postmodern Marxism." *Culture, Theory and Critique* 47, no. 2 (2006): 181–96.

Itoh, Makoto. "Money and Credit in Socialist Economies: A Reconsideration." *Capital and Class* 20, no. 3 (1996): 95–118.

Jameson, Fredric. *Representing "Capital": A Reading of Volume One.* New York: Verso, 2011.

Jorland, Gérard. "The Coming into Being and Passing Away of Value Theories in Economics (1776–1976)." In *Biographies of Scientific Objects*, edited by Lorraine Daston, 117–31. Chicago: University of Chicago Press, 2000.

Karatani, Kojin. *Transcritique: On Kant and Marx.* Cambridge: MIT Press, 2005.

Kirsch, Scott, and Don Mitchell. "The Nature of Dead Things: Dead Labor, Nonhuman Actors, and the Persistence of Marxism." *Antipode* 36 (2004): 681–699.

Kliman, Andrew. *Reclaiming Marx's "Capital."* Lanham, Md.: Lexington Books, 2006.

Lebowitz, Michael. *Beyond Capital: Marx's Political Economy of the Working Class.* New York: Palgrave Macmillan, 2003.

Lefebvre, Henri. *Critique of Everyday Life.* Vol. 2. New York: Verso, 2002.

Lenin, V. I. "Preface to the Russian Translation of Karl Marx's Letters to Dr. Kugelmann." Marxists.org. Originally published in 1907. http://www.marxists.org/archive/lenin/works/1907/feb/05.htm.

Loftus, Alex. *Everyday Environmentalism: Creating an Urban Political Ecology.* Minneapolis: University of Minnesota Press, 2012.

Macherey, Pierre. *In a Materialist Way.* New York: Verso, 1998.

Mann, Geoff. "Time, Space, and Money in Capitalism and Communism." *Human Geography* 1, no. 2 (2008): 4–12.

Marx, Karl. "Notes on Adolf Wagner." Marxists.org. Originally published in 1881. http://www.marxists.org/archive/marx/works/1881/01/wagner.htm.

———. *A Contribution to the Critique of Political Economy.* New York: International Publishers, 1970.

———. "Letter to Kugelmann, 11 July 1868." In *Karl Marx, Selected Writings*, edited by David McLellan, 524–25. Oxford: Oxford University Press, 1977.

———. "Critique of the Gotha Program." In *The Marx-Engels Reader*, 2nd ed., edited by Robert C. Tucker, 525–41. New York: Norton, 1978.

———. "Economic and Philosophic Manuscripts of 1844." In *The Marx-Engels Reader*, 2nd ed., edited by Robert C. Tucker, 66–125. New York: Norton, 1978.

———. *The German Ideology*. New York: International Publishers, 1986.

———. *Capital: A Critique of Political Economy*. Vol. 1. New York: Penguin, 1990.

———. *Capital: A Critique of Political Economy*. Vol. 3. New York: Penguin, 1991.

———. *Grundrisse: Foundations of the Critique of Political Economy*. New York: Penguin, 1993.

———. *The Poverty of Philosophy*. Amherst, N.Y.: Prometheus Books, 1995.

Marx, Karl, and F. Engels. *On the Paris Commune*. Moscow: Progress, 1971.

Massey, Doreen. "Economic: Non-economic." In *Geographies of Economies*, edited by Roger Lee and Jane Wills, 27–36. London: Edward Arnold, 1997.

Meek, Ronald. *Economics and Ideology and Other Essays: Studies in the Development of Economic Thought*. London: Chapman and Hall, 1967.

Metz, Christian. "Photography and Fetish." *October* 34 (1985): 81–90.

Miller, Daniel. "Turning Callon the Right Way Up." *Economy and Society* 31, no. 2 (2002): 218–33.

———. "The Uses of Value." *Geoforum* 39, no. 3 (2008): 1122–32.

Miller, Daniel, and James Carrier, eds. *Virtualism: A New Political Economy*. London: Berg, 1998.

Morawski, Stefan. Introduction to *Marx and Engels on Literature and Art: A Selection of Writings*, edited by Lee Baxandall and Stefan Morawski. St. Louis, Mo.: Telos Press, 1973.

Mosely, Fred, ed. *Marx's Method in "Capital": A Reexamination*. Atlantic Highlands, N.J.: Humanities Press, 1993.

Murray, Patrick. "Marx's 'Truly Social' Labor Theory of Value: Part I, Abstract Labor in Marxian Value Theory." *Historical Materialism* 6, no. 1 (2000): 27–65.

———. "Marx's 'Truly Social' Labor Theory of Value: Part II, How Is Labor that Is under the Sway of Capital Actually Abstract?" *Historical Materialism* 7, no. 1 (2000): 99–136.

Negri, Antonio. *Marx beyond Marx: Lessons on the "Grundrisse."* London: Pluto Press, 1991.

North, Peter. *Money and Liberation: The Micropolitics of Alternative Currency Movements*. Minneapolis: University of Minnesota Press, 2007.

Pels, Peter. "The Spirit of Matter: On Fetish, Rarity, Fact, and Fancy."

In *Border Fetishisms: Material Objects in Unstable Spaces*, edited by Patricia Spyer, 91–121. New York: Routledge, 1998.

Postone, Moishe. *Time, Labor, and Social Domination: A Reinterpretation of Marx's Critical Theory*. Cambridge: Cambridge University Press, 1993.

———. "Critique and Historical Transformation." *Historical Materialism* 12, no. 3 (2004): 53–72.

Rancière, Jacque. *The Philosopher and His Poor*. Durham, N.C.: Duke University Press, 2003.

Read, Jason. "Figures of the Common: Species Being, Transindividuality, Virtual Action." Paper presented at The Future of the Common: Nature, Work, and Technology, Department of Geography, University of Minnesota, September 18, 2009.

———. "The Production of Subjectivity: From Transindividuality to the Commons." *New Formations* 70 (2011): 113–31.

Roberts, Bruce. "The Visible and the Measurable." In *Postmodern Materialism and the Future of Marxist Theory: Essays in the Althusserian Tradition*, edited by Antonio Callari and David Ruccio, 193–211. Hanover, N.H.: Wesleyan University Press, 1996.

Rose, Margaret. *Marx's Lost Aesthetic: Karl Marx and the Visual Arts*. New York: Cambridge University Press, 1984.

Rubin, I. I. *Essays on Marx's Theory of Value*. Delhi: Aakar Books, 2008.

Saad-Filho, Alfredo. "Labor, Money, and 'Labor-Money': A Review of Marx's Critique of John Gray's Monetary Analysis." *History of Political Economy* 25, no. 1 (1993): 65–84.

Sartwell, Crispin. *Political Aesthetics*. Ithaca, N.Y.: Cornell University Press, 2010.

Sayers, Sean. "Creative Activity and Alienation in Hegel and Marx." *Historical Materialism* 11, no. 1 (2003): 107–28.

Sheppard, Eric, and Trevor Barnes. *The Capitalist Space Economy*. Cambridge, Mass.: Unwin Hyman, 1990.

Spivak, Gayatri. "Scattered Speculations on the Question of Value." In *In Other Worlds*, 154–75. New York: Routledge, 1988.

Storper, Michael, and Richard Walker. *The Capitalist Imperative*. Oxford: Blackwell, 1989.

Thoburn, Nicholas. "Communist Objects and the Values of Printed Matter." *Social Text 103* 28, no. 2 (2010): 1–30.

Trotsky, Leon. *Literature and Revolution*. Chicago: Haymarket Books, 2005.

Vieta, Marcelo. "The New Cooperativism." Special issue, *Affinities* (2010).

Weeks, Kathi. "Feminist Standpoint Theories and the Return of Labor." In *Marxism in the Postmodern Age: Confronting the New World Order*, edited by Antonio Callari, Stephen Cullenberg, and Carole Biewener, 292–96. New York: Guilford, 1995.

Žižek, Slajov. *Living in the End Times*. New York: Verso, 2010.

Index

abstract labor. *See* labor; value
Althusser, Louis, 18, 124, 126–27,
    136, 143, 150n2, 150n5,
    158n36
art, 158n38; Marx and, 129–36,
    158n32; social relations and,
    xvi–xviii, 126–47
associated production: limits of,
    xiv–xviii, xxiv–xxv, 79–83,
    87–88, 118–26; specter of, in
    capitalist value, xxiii–xxiv, 18,
    59–61, 63–65, 68–71, 73–75,
    77–79, 85–88

Balibar, Étienne, 127
Barnes, Trevor, 28, 151n16,
    153n3
Bauman, Zygmunt, 14, 156n14

Caffentzis, George, 155n3
capital. *See* value
Capital, volume 1 (Marx), xvii,
    xxii, 1–34, 99, 122. *See also*
    commodity fetish
Capital, volume 3 (Marx),
    xxiii–xxiv; associated produc-
    tion in, 59–88, 153–54n3
Casarino, Cesare, 90–91, 103,
    155n2
Castree, Noel, 18, 150n2
Clarke, David, 14, 145
Cleaver, Harry, 52–53, 152n3
commodity fetish, 9–18, 151n10;

radicalization of, xvi–xviii,
    122–26, 128–36, 140–47
common, 90–91, 114–15
communism. *See* associated
    production
credit, 72–75
Critique of the Gotha Program
    (Marx), 100, 158n30

De Angelis, Massimo, 151n10
Deleuze, Gilles, and Félix Guat-
    tari, 125, 143
Doel, Marcus, 34

Eagleton, Terry, 129–30, 138–39,
    157n20
*Economic and Philosophic
    Manuscripts of 1844, The*
    (Marx), 118–26, 143
Eighteenth Brumaire (Marx),
    130, 138, 142
Elson, Diane, xix–xx, 151n10
Engels, Friedrich, 60–61,
    52–53n8
estrangement, 119–20; value of,
    140–47
exchange value. *See* value

fetish. *See* commodity fetish
Foucault, Michel, 82, 140, 158n36

Gibson-Graham, J. K., 150n3
Gidwani, Vinay, xxiii, 117, 127

George Henderson is associate professor of geography at the University of Minnesota. He is the author of *California and the Fictions of Capital* and coeditor of *Geographic Thought: A Praxis Perspective.*